THE WELL-CONNECTED COMMUNITY

A networking approach to community development

Alison Gilchrist

The POLICY

P~P

P R E S S

COMMUNITY
DEVELOPMENT
FOUNDATION

First published in Great Britain in January 2004 by

The Policy Press
University of Bristol
Fourth Floor
Beacon House
Queen's Road
Bristol BS8 1QU
UK

Tel +44 (0)117 331 4054
Fax +44 (0)117 331 4093
e-mail tpp-info@bristol.ac.uk
www.policypress.org.uk

British Library Cataloguing in Publication Data
A catalogue record for this book is available from the British Library.

Library of Congress Cataloging-in-Publication Data
A catalog record for this book has been requested.

ISBN 1 86134 527 5 paperback

Alison Gilchrist is Director of Practice Development at the Community Development Foundation and a Visiting Research Fellow at the University of the West of England, Bristol.

Cover design by Qube Design Associates, Bristol.
Front cover: aerial view supplied by kind permission of Getmapping.com plc
Printed and bound in Great Britain by Bell & Bain Ltd, Glasgow.

Contents

List of tables, figures and boxes

Tables

Figure

Boxes

Foreword

I am delighted to have the opportunity to introduce Alison's book. Communities and networks are at the centre of government policy as this book is published. But Alison was thinking about networks well before it became fashionable to do so. And like a good networker, she was also making connections across conventional disciplinary boundaries to explain what she saw out in the communities where she worked. So, while this book is well grounded in practice, it also provides us with new ways of looking at how communities work and links theory convincingly and helpfully into practice.

The well-connected community provides a much-needed and very thorough analysis of community development, in a field that has lacked theoretical development for a long time. Having had the benefit of reading it as it developed, I have already used it in my own work and I know others have as well. It is good to see it out in the public domain at last and I am sure that both practitioners and scholars will find it immensely useful.

Marilyn Taylor
September 2003

Preface

The naturalist John Muir once wrote "when we try to pick out anything by itself, we find it hitched to everything else in the universe" and this has certainly been my experience of thinking, researching and writing about networking. My initial interest in networking emerged from my experience as a neighbourhood community worker and political activist. I became aware of how useful it is to have a range of connections in terms of getting things done without many resources and without much obvious power or status. I also noticed that keeping this web of contacts and relationships required quite a lot of time and some ingenuity, and that the women I knew were particularly adept and committed to this way of working. I began to realise that networking was not only an efficient approach to developing collective action, but represented an aspect of work that was insufficiently rewarded. I was motivated by a desire to find out why and how networking enabled people to work together to achieve their common goals. What makes a good networker? Why are networks so useful? These were the key questions that led me into an investigation of the skills and strategies that underpin both effective and ethical networking.

The findings described in the book are based on research undertaken to discover how networking is used by community workers and others to develop collective action among communities and to underpin multi-agency working. I was particularly interested in the tactics and traits that good networkers demonstrated, and wanted to make more visible the skilled and strategic nature of *good* networking. The research programme consisted of two parts. The first was a case study of my own involvement in coordinating the first Bristol Festival Against Racism in 1994. The second phase of the research involved working with a panel of community practitioners over 12 months. They were asked to identify key networks in their professional practice and describe what they were used for, as well as any limitations. The community workers then spent a few weeks making notes of 'critical incidents' that had occurred in their professional or private lives that they felt had contributed in some way to community development. The evidence collected from these two stages was used to construct the questions for one-to-one interviews and the whole process culminated in a focus group discussion in which panelists considered the research findings and debated implications for community development policies and practice.

This book is not, however, just based on the research. Over the past decade or so I have enjoyed numerous discussions and workshops with people involved in community development. These have contributed immensely to my learning and have encouraged me to turn a rather academic thesis into what I hope is a practical and stimulating book.

Acknowledgements

It would be invidious (and impossible) to name everyone who has contributed to the writing of this book since so many people from so many of my networks have added something.

But it is important to acknowledge the reflective and dedicated input from the people I surveyed and interviewed for the two studies. They are:

Bristol Festival Against Racism: Balraj Sandhu, Mike Graham, Rosetta Eligon, Ray Safia, Minoo Jalali, Steve Graham, Richard Jewison, Jane Kilpatrick, Lindy Clifton, Peter Courtier, Lil Bowers, Batook Pandya

Members of the Panel Study: Frances Brown, Teri Dolan, Pete Hulse, Caroline Kay, John Mayhew, Linda McMann, Susan Moores, Anne Pendleton, Gary Smith, Greg Smith, Keib Thomas, Chris Trueblood, Mike Waite.

I would also like to thank colleagues at the Community Development Foundation and the Standing Conference for Community Development for their continuing encouragement and support. The Faculty of Health and Social Care at the University of the West of England (Bristol) funded and supported the research for my PhD, and I am grateful to colleagues there for their advice and interest. My advisors at the University of Bristol were Marilyn Taylor, Linda Martin and Danny Burns. This book would be much poorer without their challenging questions and advice.

Finally, I appreciate the chivvying, distractions and faith offered by my family and friends that have kept me going over the past few years.

ONE

The meaning and value of community networks

When the stranger says: what is the meaning of this city?
Do you huddle together because you love each other?
What will you answer?
'We all dwell together to make money from each other'?
or 'This is a community'? (T.S. Eliot, *The chorus of the rocks*)

Introduction

Community development is fundamentally about the development of 'community' and it therefore makes sense to begin by examining what we know and understand about the idea. This book is based on a belief that the most important aspects of community are the informal networks that exist between people, between groups and between organisations. Community provides a crucial dimension to our lives and is a persistent theme within policy making. This chapter considers some of the advantages and limitations of community networks; for individuals, for society as a whole and for government programmes. It looks briefly at evidence and theories from anthropology and sociology concerning community life, explores the modern concept of social capital, before setting out the ways in which networks operate to the benefit of communities and conversely, the ways in which they distort or suppress choices and opportunities. The model of the 'well-connected community' presented in this book argues that community development has a role to play in helping people to make connections that are useful and empowering, and, in particular, overcoming or renegotiating some of the obstacles that prevent people from communicating and cooperating with one another. First, however, what contribution do networks make to community life? What have community studies revealed about people's everyday interactions and relationships? How is the term 'community' used and how does it compare to the idea of 'social capital'? What relevance does all this have for public policy and social welfare?

Anthropological research shows that community-type organisation is a feature of all human societies and studies of humans and other higher primates suggest that we share an inherent sociability, a willingness to connect and to cooperate. Indeed it has been suggested that this ability to coordinate activities with people beyond the immediate family group was what gave homo sapiens an evolutionary advantage over Neanderthals in the struggle for survival in the harsh climate of the European ice age over 30,000 years ago (Dunbar, 1996; Gamble, 1999). Nevertheless, community has proved notoriously difficult to define and to study. In his now classic trawl through definitions of community, Hillery (1955) identified a core feature of regular, mostly cooperative interactions among a set of people over time. Calling a set of people a 'community' generally implies that they have some common characteristic or bond (Taylor et al, 2000). It also raises expectations of loyalty, support, social cohesion and affirmation. Most people regard community as a 'good thing' and we often hear a nostalgic lament that 'community' is disappearing from modern lives and needs to be reinvigorated, and possibly even reinvented. Indeed, this is the main rationale for community development. This quest for community has been around for over a century and has been the focus of much research and debate. Early sociologists such as Tönnies (1887) and Durkheim (1893) emphasised the emotional aspects of local life, arguing that common experiences, shared values and mutuality were key features that distinguish *Gemeinschaft* (community) from *Gesellschaft* (society). Tönnies contrasted community with the public, commercial sphere of society, while Durkheim argued that community represented a form of 'organic solidarity', based on resemblance and shared fate. This distinction inspired a whole research field known as community studies (cf Nisbet, 1953; Bell and Newby, 1971; Crow and Allan, 1994). Usually these involved detailed observations of "ordinary people's everyday lives" (Crow and Allan, 1994, p xiv), elaborated through conversations with community members in order to identify and analyse patterns of interaction and attachment.

Aspects of community

Initially, community studies focused on specific localities, reporting on how institutions and traditions shaped community life. The geographical dimension of community was paramount in defining the set of people studied, such as the residents of a particular neighbourhood, small town or island (Frankenburg, 1966). Locality was seen as an important dimension of people's identity and sense of belonging, and there was a strong emphasis in these studies on the positive aspects of community life – the solidarity, the mutual support and the ways in which people cooperated as part of their routine activities. This model of community still holds sway in many people's minds and has strongly influenced government area-based initiatives and some aspects of the neighbourhood renewal strategy (NRU, 2002).

However, studies soon revealed that social networks extend beyond geographical boundaries, often based around work, faith or people's hobbies (Webber, 1963; Wellman, 1979). Moreover, communities can be regarded as actively constructed by their members, not merely arising from local circumstances. Cultural traditions and symbols are used to assert or imagine community identity, expressed through ritual activities, music and flags, or their equivalent (Anderson, 1983; Cohen, 1986; Back, 1996). This is about conventions and customs, often linked to religious or sporting occasions, but also about the ways in which people go about their everyday lives – their hairstyles, dress codes, their language and so on. Such 'badges of belonging' reinforce community boundaries and can help identify 'friends' and 'allies'.

Community networks enhance people's ability to cope with difficulties and disasters. Sharing scarce resources during times of hardship is common among communities living in poverty or harsh environments, and can be crucial to the survival of some community members. Studies of communities hit by a shared catastrophe, such as a rock slide or long strike action, suggest that those with strong social networks are able to recover more quickly than those where networks are obliterated or non-existent (Erikson, 1979; Waddington et al, 1991; Marris, 1996). The support and practical help provided by social networks appear to help both at an individual and a community level. As well as communities appearing to crystallise from sudden disaster, they also coalesce around experiences of systematic discrimination and exclusion. This has been especially important in situations where communities have been disrupted by civil war or migration (Hall, 1990). Sivanandan (1990), writing about the struggles of Black and minority ethnic communities in Britain, calls these 'communities of resistance', similar in purpose to the array of self-help groups and buddying arrangements that sprang up within gay communities to cope with the HIV/AIDS crisis (Sullivan, 1998). These "networks of necessity" (Hunter and Staggenborg, 1988, p 253) are crucial mechanisms for the survival and sustenance of poor and other oppressed groups. They comprise communities of shared interest or political identity.

Forming communities of identity or shared interest can thus be seen as a device for collective empowerment and is a familiar strategy for countering the dimensions of oppression associated with 'race', gender, disability, age and sexual orientation (for example, Hall and Jefferson, 1975; Gilroy, 1982; Weeks, 1990; Morris, 1991). This political dimension of 'community' articulates a particular perspective or 'consciousness' developed through processes of reflection and debate (such as the women's groups of the 1970s). It finds expression in notions of 'pride' (such as Gay Pride or the Notting Hill carnival), the self-organisation of Disabled people (Morris, 1991) or through an exploration of historical 'roots' (Ohri, 1998). These actions provide opportunities for people to maintain a sense of collective identity in a hostile world by demanding that "difference not merely be tolerated and accepted, but that it is valued and celebrated" (Oliver, 1996, p 89). The resulting social networks reinforce a sense of community and provide a vital foundation for collective action, especially where this is risky or highly demanding as is often the case when challenging injustice or exploitation. Solidarity in the face of adversity or injustice is an important facet of community, but this same sense of 'us' versus 'them' can lead to sectarian violence and the segregation of minority groups.

The importance of diversity is well understood in southern and eastern cultures. Gandhi insisted "civilisation is the celebration of differences". There is an African saying that 'It takes a whole village to raise a child' and an Akan proverb contends that 'in a single polis there is no wisdom' (Appiah, 1999). Within communities, diversity can be enriching and dynamic, but it also needs careful attention, particularly where inequalities and incompatibilities generate unease and misunderstanding. Strains and conflicts are inherent within communities, even where there is an appearance of unity (Brent, 1997). The reality of community life encompasses many different identities and allegiances making up a kaleidoscope of intersecting layers of experience and expectations that characterise people's real lives, their histories, current preoccupations, enthusiasms and future aspirations. Occasionally, these incompatibilities and rivalries emerge as inter-communal tensions, flaring up as gang warfare or so-called 'race' riots. Communities become fractured with networks that stop short at ethnic or other 'identity' boundaries. Social cohesion is undermined in a twisting spiral of mutual suspicion and competition for what are often scarce resources. In these situations where communities feel under attack, they can become polarised and defensive, attempting to stem the tide of integration or to reclaim cultural traditions.

Many people feel they belong to several communities simultaneously. Their networks are flexible and strategic, depending on the social and political context, as well as their personal circumstances and choices. In this post-modern view of social identity (Rutherford, 1990; Squires, 1994), community takes on a hybrid form, containing contradictory and reflexive features that flow through people's lives, mingling different aspects of their experience and affiliations. The predominantly Western model of the free and independent individual seems strange to other cultures that have a more collectivist way of life and find great value in the web of relationships that connect people to places and to each other. For example, the Xhosa principle of 'ubuntu' conveys the meaning 'I am because we are'. As Archbishop Tutu explained, "It embraces hospitality, caring about others.... We believe a person is a person through another person, that my humanity is caught up, bound up and inextricable in yours" (cited in du Toit, 1998, p 89).

Social capital and community

As Williams (1976, p 65) noted, the term 'community' remains a "warmly persuasive word ... [that] never seems to be used unfavourably". In this respect, it has similar connotations to the more modern, and currently popular term, social capital, first coined by Harifan (1916), and transformed from metaphor to concept (Field, 2003), most notably by Jacobs (1961), Coleman (1988, 1990), Bourdieu (1986), Putnam (1993, 2000) and Woolcock (1998, 2001). Broadly speaking, social capital can be defined as a collective asset made up of social networks based on shared norms of trust and mutuality. Jacobs (1961) referred to a "web of public respect ... [which constituted] a resource in times of personal or neighbourhood need". Social capital recognises that relationships between neighbours, colleagues, friends, even casual acquaintances, have value for the individual and for society as a whole. Coleman was particularly interested in how these affected children's development and their educational attainment. His research indicated that young people with strong experiences of family and community tended to do well at school. Shared expectations of reciprocity and mutual obligation created a general bias towards cooperation. Coleman believed that social capital accumulated as a result of beneficial exchanges and interaction between people pursuing their own self-interest rather than as a deliberate investment strategy. For Coleman, the norms embedded in these community networks could counteract possible disadvantages associated with socio-economic background (Coleman, 1988, 1990) and he therefore saw social capital as an unmitigated public good that had wide implications for public policy.

The French sociologist, Bourdieu, was more critical of the function of social capital in society because he was concerned with how inequalities in wealth and power were perpetuated through culture and connections (1986, 1993). He was influenced by neo-Marxist theories concerning the class structure of society, but was also interested in how social interactions affect people's access to resources and status. Bourdieu's view was that social capital was a source of privilege that benefited the upper echelons, but had little relevance for other sections of society except to exclude them from opportunities for advancement. This notion of elite networks based on 'who we know and how we use them' (Heald, 1983) will be explored further in Chapter Four. Bourdieu and other neo-Marxist writers (for example, Baum, 2000, Fine, 2000) emphasise the importance of economic and social forces in the maintenance of social capital that, it is argued, interact with other forms of capital, notably financial and cultural. Others have raised questions about gender dynamics and the well-documented contribution that women make to community life (Forrest and Kearns, 1999; Lowndes, 2000). Hall's (2000) work on social capital in Britain suggests that there is a class factor, with middle-class people being more likely to be members of voluntary or civic associations while working-class households enjoy higher levels of informal sociability.

Putnam is generally credited with popularising the concept of social capital and highlighting its implications for government (ONS, 2001; PIU, 2002). His more liberal approach has a particular resonance with communitarian models of social and family responsibility and therefore has wide appeal to New Labour politicians and policy makers. Putnam describes social capital as the "connections among individuals – social networks and the norms of reciprocity and trustworthiness that arise from them" (2000, p 19) that are created and maintained through voluntary associations, civic life and community activity. Putnam's research on levels of social capital, initially in Italy but more recently in the US, appears to demonstrate strong correlations with economic prosperity, stable governance and social cohesion (1993, 1995, 2001). This has understandably attracted interest from a wide range of national and global agencies concerned with economic development and political stability. The World Bank has been especially keen to invest in programmes that build social capital in the developing world as a strategy for combating poverty and supporting regeneration (Narayan and Pritchett, 1997; Woolcock, 1998).

Putnam acknowledges that social capital is closely related to our experience of community, reflecting levels of general trust and inter-connectivity within society. Just like the concept of community, it reflects shared norms and values, affirmed through sustained interaction and cooperation. Putnam and his followers, therefore, promote increased volunteering and active citizenship as the means to reverse an apparent decline in social capital in Western countries. In community development, we might argue that encouraging greater participation in community activities of all kinds would have the same effect, including involvement in civic associations and public partnerships. Much of the literature on social capital emphasises trust as a component of "the ability of people to work together for common purpose in groups and organisations" (Fukuyama, 1996, p 10). Trust implies both an expectation of mutual commitment and a degree of predictability about other people's behaviour. But trust is not just an aspect of social relationships. It is context-dependent, reflecting differential power and access to independent resources, as well as an ability (or not) to apply sanctions (Foley and Edwards, 1999). For communities, trust is a complicated process, requiring respect and a collective accountability on the part of leaders, partners and participants (Purdue, 2001). While the concept of trust has seen a welcome revival in discussions around policy and practice, it is perhaps most useful to regard social capital as "quintessentially a product of collective interaction" (Field, 2003, p 20). It is the value added through networking processes, and resides within the web of ties and linkages that we call community.

Of course, a web is only a metaphor and social networks are by no means uniform in their structure and configurations. As we shall examine more closely in Chapter Three, the threads that connect people vary in strength, directionality and density. Woolcock (2001), echoing Granovetter's (1973) distinction between 'strong' and 'weak' ties, suggested that there are different kinds of social capital:

- *bonding:* based on enduring, multi-faceted relationships between similar people with strong mutual commitments such as among friends, family and other close-knit groups;
- *bridging:* formed from the connections between people who have less in common, but may have an overlapping interest, for example, between neighbours, colleagues, or between different groups within a community; and
- *linking:* derived from the links between people or organisations beyond peer boundaries, cutting across status and similarity and enabling people to exert influence and reach resources outside their normal circles.

Each of these is necessary for strong and sustainable communities, but community development is primarily concerned with the latter two forms of social capital. Bridging capital can be seen as important for managing diversity and maintaining community cohesion. Linking capital is needed for empowerment and partnership working. The networking approach used to develop the 'well-connected community' emphasises the role played by community workers in helping people to build bridges and make links that they might otherwise find difficult.

The benefits of community networks

Although the idea of 'community as social capital' begs many questions (Taylor, 2003), community does seem to represent a significant collective resource. Many people get involved in community activities in order to meet people and gain a sense of belonging. For some, this is about self-help and community campaigns in order to cope during times of adversity and to secure a decent quality of life for themselves and their families. Community networks supply practical assistance with a variety of tasks (Williams and Windebank, 1995, 2000). They operate as a collective mechanism for sharing risk and resources in situations of scarcity and uncertainty (Stack, 1974; Werbner, 1988). Small and routine acts of neighbourliness maintain loose ties within localities, improving people's sense of safety and strengthening community cohesion (Ball and Ball, 1982; Henning and Lieberg, 1996). Participation in community life takes many forms and is shaped by a variety of motivations and emotions. It is essentially voluntary, dependent on circumstances, preferences and access to resources. Such informal transactions retain a balance of reciprocity over time, and there have been attempts in recent years to formalise these arrangements through community-based 'care and share' schemes, such as LETS (Local Exchange Trading Schemes) in which skills are swapped for tokens or Time Banks where the currency is measured in units of time (Williams et al, 2001; Seyfang and Smith, 2002; Burns et al, 2004). Proponents of these rather artificial mechanisms claim that they can be used to re-create community spirit and they have attracted interest (and some funding) from government and regeneration agencies. These moneyless economies provide vital sources of assistance and support, especially within impoverished communities who cannot resort to the 'market' to meet their needs.

The personal relationships and social networks established and nurtured through community activities appear to bring considerable benefits in terms of people's well-being (Pilisuk and Parks, 1986). Informal conversations within trusting relationships provide information and advice on various matters. Community networks act as cheap and user-friendly referral systems (Hornby, 1993), supplying help at times of crisis and are often resorted to before professional (sometimes stigmatised) help is requested from the appropriate agencies, particularly about embarrassing or risky problems (Gabarino, 1983). Having knowledgeable people within one's social network is useful, assuming of course that such enquiries will be treated in confidence and not form the basis for gossip or disapproval. Social networks supply informal care (Bulmer, 1987), although family and friends provide different kinds of support compared to neighbours, a fact that was somewhat overlooked by 'care in the community' strategies. In addition to these practical benefits, social networks have an emotional impact. Social psychologists have studied happiness and conclude that social interaction of almost any kind tends to make people happy, both in the short term but also in terms of their general disposition (Argyle, 1989). It appears that it is not only the quality of social interaction that has this effect, but also the quantity. People with diverse networks (maintained through a variety of activities) seem to exist on a higher level of contentment than those with an intensely supportive, but homogenous set of relationships (Argyle, 1996a, 1996b; Ornish, 1999). This also applies to reported levels of health in that individuals with robust and diverse networks lead healthier lives than those who are more isolated or whose networks consist of similar people (Flynn, 1989; Yen and Syme, 1999). They have stronger immune systems, suffer less from heart disease, recover more quickly from emotional trauma and seem to be more resistant to the debilitating effects of illness, possibly because of a generally positive outlook or because they maintain a more active lifestyle (Pilisuk and Parks, 1986; Blane et al, 1996; Kawachi, 1996).

Community networks of informal relationships make it easier for people to communicate and cooperate with one another. They create the conditions for collective action, enabling people to work together to achieve (or defend) shared interests. Those communities that are 'well-connected' have an advantage when it comes to organising themselves for whatever purpose. This might be informal arrangements for childcare, or semi-formal lending circles, such as the pardoner system brought over by African Caribbean communities and used to smooth their settlement in Britain. The Pakistani clan-like *biraderi* offered similar networks of support to newly arrived migrants and continue to exert their influence on patterns of loyalty and exchange (Werbner, 1990; Anwar, 1995). Community networks enable people to mobilise for campaigns and events, pooling effort and resources for collective benefit and shared goals. They become a repository of 'common sense' and local knowledge, acting as a source of wisdom, information and 'gossip' (Tebbutt, 1995). As Smith recognised:

> Experienced community workers develop the art of 'jizz' over time and find it invaluable. Intimate knowledge based on networking covers such areas as who gets on with whom, who used to work for which organisation and why the director of one local organisation has the ears of the chair of social services. Gossip is among the most precious information in community work. Such material is too sensitive and too complex to store on a computer ... what a competent community worker carries in her head is a highly sophisticated relational database. (1999, p 13)

Maintaining connections with different sources within and beyond the community is a form of intelligence gathering, enabling people to gain access to advice, services and resources that they might not otherwise know about or be able to influence. Gossip is also a way of learning from different experiences, generating new ideas and insights (Yerkovich, 1977). In this respect, the 'community' dimension of society can be seen as a mechanism for integration and cohesion. It creates arenas in which differences are acknowledged rather than feared or reviled. Ideally, community offers a simple affirmation of similarity and mutuality, in which diversity can flourish and individual relationships form (Jenkins, 1996). In Britain, recent debates around nationality, citizenship and community cohesion have struggled to identify what constitutes 'belonging' and 'common values' (Rattansi, 2002; Modood, 2003). One solution is to recognise the existence (and value) of a "community of communities", such as proposed in the report, *The future of multi-racial Britain* (Parekh, 2000, p 56).

Problems of community

However, 'community' also has a downside and informal networks can be notoriously private and opaque (Taylor, 2003). Relationships are not always universally beneficial, either for the individual or for society as a whole. Communities are sometimes elitist, 'tribalist' and oppressive. The dominant norms associated with strong communities may be damaging to the confidence and identity of anyone whose preferences or activities deviate from the defined 'standard' of acceptable behaviour. Consequently, people who cannot, or do not want to fit in with this framework of what is deemed 'right and proper' either pretend to conform or are ostracised. Community-based sanctions are applied to uphold shared conventions and perpetuate stereotypes, including malicious rumour, 'sending to Coventry', and at one extreme, vigilante activities and lynchings. Social networks are used to exert these pressures, causing misery as well as bodily harm.

Peer pressure can hold people back, outweighing scientific knowledge and personal belief systems, to overturn long-term benefits and aspirations. We see this in relation to the smoking habits of young people, and patterns of truancy and petty vandalism. Adults are also susceptible, finding themselves influenced by the ideas, choices and behaviour of friends, colleagues and neighbours, sometimes against their own better judgement. Criminal and paedophile rings operate in this way, justifying their activities only by comparison to other network members, rather than against wider social norms. Corruption likewise depends on closed networks and misguided loyalties. Communities that are closed to outside influence and scrutiny may become stagnant and isolated from the rest of society. Furthermore, networks often contain pockets of power that are difficult to unmask or challenge. As Freeman (1973) noted in her essay on the 'tyranny of structurelessness' within the women's liberation movement, informality can become a "smokescreen for the strong or the lucky to establish unquestioned hegemony over others" (p 1). Inequalities between network members can undermine the reciprocity that is needed to sustain relationships and may provide a systematic advantage for a specific clique. This is both unjust and inefficient because it fails to harness or fairly reward ability. Because networks can operate to restrict opportunity and merit, a networking approach to community development must be proactive in countering and overcoming barriers set up through personal friendships and prejudices.

Community as a dimension of policy

Despite these drawbacks, there has been a resurgent interest in the idea of community among academics, policy makers and politicians (Hoggett, 1997; Taylor, 2003). This is true of Britain in the 21st century but has implications and a resonance way beyond this country (see for example, Craig and Mayo, 1995). In the past the prefix 'community' has been used to soften the edge of state interventions, implying user-friendly, accessible services or partnership arrangements for the delivery of welfare to those sections of the population said to have needs that are particularly difficult to meet. Consequently, when used as a collective noun, 'community' tends to refer to people who are disadvantaged by poverty, oppression and prejudice. It has been noted that in public policy discussions, we rarely hear about middle-class communities and this is certainly true of recent pronouncements on social inclusion strategies (Levitas, 1998). Communitarian thinking prescribes stable and well-integrated communities as a condition for progress, particularly when faced with complex and intractable problems (Henderson and Salmon, 1998). It has been argued that by promoting community involvement as a palliative (if not a cure) for 'social exclusion', governments are seeking to avoid demands for significant redistribution of resources and opportunities.

There are three strands to the government's current concern with 'community':

- social capital;
- governance; and
- service delivery.

High levels of *social capital* appear to be correlated with several core policy objectives around improving health, reducing crime, increasing educational attainment and economic regeneration. Given the evidence linking social networks to these policy outcomes, it makes sense for the government to support interventions that strengthen networks and build trust (Halpern, 2004: in press). New, more participative forms of *governance* are being developed that rely on active citizenship, multi-agency partnerships in which communities are strongly represented as stakeholders and local 'experts' (Stewart, 2000). In terms of *service delivery*, community groups and voluntary organisations provide significant forms of self-help and informal support. The voluntary and community sector, in particular, has been influential in pioneering welfare services tailored to the needs of specific sections of the population that have been overlooked by mainstream agencies. The recruitment and support of volunteers has also been a major function of the sector, running local and community activities in addition to providing auxiliary services in public institutions such as hospitals or schools. Many current policies and programmes see 'community' as an arena of rights and obligations, expressed through acts of citizenship and volunteering, rather than a foundation for collective organising. A welcome exception to this is the recent Home Office report on *Building civil renewal*, which asserts the value of participation in community activities in building social networks and strengthening organisational infrastructure (RCU, 2003b). The theme of community involvement, alongside communitarian notions of social responsibility, runs throughout modern urban and public policies (Butcher et al, 1993; Mayo, 1994; Chanan, 2003; Nash and Christie, 2003). Increasingly, social networks are recognised as crucial to the capacity of communities to participate in, and even deliver government initiatives (6, 2002; Taylor, 2003).

Community networks provide important infrastructure capacity within civil society. They have a particular relevance to policies and programmes seeking to promote democratic renewal, social cohesion, regeneration and public health. The government's commitment to community involvement and partnership working represents a genuine and constructive attempt to transform public planning and service delivery. In order to turn the rhetoric of community empowerment and community leadership into a meaningful and sustainable reality, informal and formal networks must be developed and strengthened so that representatives can be supported and held accountable. Similarly, time and effort is needed to build relationships of trust and respect across different sectors and between partner agencies responsible for designing and managing the new plans or strategies.

Community development can be seen as building or releasing social capital for collective benefit. It supports networks that foster mutual learning and develop shared commitments and a common vision so that people can work and live together in relatively stable communities. The purpose of community development is to maintain and renew 'community' as a foundation for the emergence of diverse initiatives and identities that are independent of both the public and private sectors. This book aims to persuade policy makers and practitioners who are responsible for community involvement that networking is a necessary and effective method of building bridging and linking social capital. It goes on to argue that a core, but hitherto neglected function of community development is to facilitate these processes by establishing and nurturing the crucial but more difficult boundary-spanning ties that support collective action and empowerment. The next chapter outlines the history and different models of community development in the UK. Chapters Three and Four consider theories about the structure and function of networks, drawing on evidence from organisational studies, psychology, political theory and network analysis, to examine how they support collective action and community leadership. Chapters Five and Six present findings from recent research into how people involved in community development use networking skills and strategies in their practice. Chapter Seven presents the 'well-connected community' model as a way of managing complex social systems, suggesting that networks offer a means of operating at the 'edge of chaos'. The book concludes with chapters that draw out implications for policy and practice, and recommend that greater attention needs to be given to networking aspects of community development.

Community development

> "There is no greater service than to help a community to liberate itself."
> (Nelson Mandela, 2003)

Chapter Two provides an overview of community development, focusing on its evolution as a form of professional intervention. It traces the history of community development over the 20th century, and examines recent applications of core methods and values in relation to a number of government programmes. The role of community workers in supporting networks is briefly highlighted, in preparation for a more detailed consideration in the following chapters.

In 1955 the United Nations referred to "Community development [as] a process designed to create conditions of economic and social progress for the whole community with its active participation". The definition captured an approach to working with people that can be used across all countries of the world. It recognised the position of many underdeveloped nations that were on the brink of independence and urgently needed to establish basic infrastructure for transport, welfare, water and so on. In the developed world the situation is different in that for most people these basics are available, even if access to services is not always straightforward or satisfactory. Community development in the UK has tended to emphasise a more general approach to strengthening community capacity and tackling broader issues around equality and social justice. Processes and principles are regarded as paramount and this is reflected through an emphasis on working *with*, rather than *for* people. The current position of community development within government policy and programmes, focused primarily on community involvement, is a continuation of past attempts to promote participation and partnership in public decision making and service delivery.

A brief historical overview

In the UK, community development derives its inspiration and rationale from three traditions each of which are at least a century old. The first of these is *informal self-help and solidarity*, the reciprocal support and sharing that characterise small-scale forms of social organisation, for example, the kind of neighbourly help that is routinely available or that emerges in times of adversity. The second strand represents a more organised form of *mutual aid*, whereby formal associations were established to provide assistance and shared resources across a defined subscriber membership. Collective organisations such as the early craft guilds, friendly societies and trades unions are examples of these. The third strand differs from the others in that it is based rather more on notions of *philanthropy and voluntary service*, expressed as a desire to improve the lives and opportunities of others deemed 'less fortunate'.

Some aspects of community development were explicitly remedial, designed to tackle what were seen as deficits in poor communities preventing residents from achieving their potential or participating properly in opportunities for personal advancement and democratic engagement. The work of the University Settlements is representative of this approach, combining adult education with 'character-building' activities and a somewhat condescending approach to the relief of hardship (Barnett, 1888, 1904; Clarke, 1963; Leat, 1975). Although the pioneers of the Settlement movement clearly stated their belief that people living in the Settlements (usually university students on temporary placements) would learn as much from local residents as vice versa, the underlying ethos was patronising and management of the Settlements' resources (buildings, workers and funds) remained in the hands of well-meaning outsiders for many decades.

Community development has also been used as a preventative strategy, intervening in situations to avert potential crises or to address issues before they become conflicts. During the rehousing programmes after the two world wars, whole communities were fractured or relocated causing widespread disruption and alienation. Community workers were employed in the New Towns and on peripheral estates to arrange events that would foster a sense of community and to encourage residents to organise activities for themselves (Goetschius, 1969; Heraud, 1975). These workers were frequently employed by social services or housing departments and saw themselves as 'agents' of the state, acting on behalf of the relevant authority rather than the local residents. Nevertheless they played an important role in managing the links within and between groups and external bodies to improve social welfare through the establishment of autonomous voluntary groups. During the 1950s and 1960s community work described itself as the preventative branch of social work, emphasising both individual development and collective welfare. The 'community' was seen as offering some protection from the impersonal institutions of the modern state and providing opportunities for democratic participation. Early writers advocated non-directive methods of intervention (Batten, 1957, 1962; Biddle and Biddle, 1965; Batten and Batten, 1967) and a new profession gradually emerged that combined two related approaches. The first saw the community as a resource, a partner, in the provision of welfare services. Problems could be addressed by involving local residents in developing collective solutions. As well as supplying volunteer staff, community associations and other locally based voluntary organisations were seen as potential managers of projects supplying social care for older people, health education, benefits advice and childcare (Reinold, 1974; Clarke, 1990). The second approach was similar, but placed more emphasis on personal fulfilment, regarding community involvement as a vehicle for self-improvement. Taking part in community activities was seen as therapeutic (staving off mental health problems), morally worthy (encouraging mutuality and social responsibility) and educational (promoting the acquisition of skills and new understandings). Adult education classes and cultural societies were seen as 'improving' in themselves, while recreational activities such as youth clubs and sports associations were encouraged as a means of diverting people from a life of crime, idleness and social isolation.

In the 1970s and 1980s community development in the UK was strongly influenced by a radical model that saw community activism as an extension of the class struggle. Some community workers sought to build alliances with the labour movement through trades councils and a chain of resource centres, specifically set up to support local campaigns. The radical model recognised that sometimes a more adversarial approach was needed; for example, when a community wanted to campaign against some kind of threat or achieve a positive change that is opposed or obstructed by those with the money and power. Citizen action models, such as Alinsky's community organising approach, tried to challenge existing power structures by mobilising residents around issues that brought them into conflict with economic interests or state institutions (Alinsky, 1969, 1972).

A Marxist analysis of the impact of modern capitalism on working-class neighbourhoods became highly influential in Britain in the 1970s, mainly through the fieldwork and research reports of the Community Development Projects (CDP, 1974, 1977; Mayo, 1975; Specht, 1976) and a series of essay collections published by the Association of Community Workers (ACW). For those on this radical wing, community work was seen as contributing to the fight for socialism, through local, militant community action (Baine, 1974; Fleetwood and Lambert, 1982). Community workers were active on issues that had a particular focus on the level and distribution of the 'social wage', through campaigns to defend or increase the quantity and quality of state welfare provision (for example, O'Malley, 1977; Corrigan and Leonard, 1978). There were increasing demands for the democratisation of the 'local state' (Lees and Mayo, 1984) and this led to a belated recognition that the role of the community worker as an agent of change 'in and against the state' generated contradictory accountabilities (LEWRG, 1979). The call to pursue confrontational and subversive tactics (Cowley, 1977; Loney, 1983) required an explicit rejection of the idea that the community worker was a neutral agent even when employed by the local council (Filkin and Naish, 1982).

The more radical workers saw community politics primarily as a means for raising 'class' (and subsequently gender) consciousness outside the workplace. Community organising was about laying the foundations for a revolutionary grassroots democracy (Tasker, 1975). This involved equipping people with the skills, knowledge, confidence and political 'nous' for challenging the root causes of poverty and discrimination (Kay, 1974). More recent versions of this approach have asserted the transformative nature of democratic participation as a form of radical empowerment (Ledwith, 1997; Craig, 1998) and the means by which many different forms of oppression and inequality can be overcome (Dominelli,

1990). Shaw and Martin regard actions by people in their communities as the "essence of democracy" and consider community workers as "key agents in re-making the vital connections between community work, citizenship and democracy" (2000, p 412). Modern broad-based organising strategies have adopted this approach but are highly critical of the role played by community development professionals (Furbey et al, 1997).

Alongside the radical community work that was undertaken in the 1970s and 1980s, the more liberal approach continued, preferring to win small gains that improved life for some people rather than taking on the whole world (Twelvetrees, 1982). This model assumes a pluralist model of society in which competing interests vie with one another to persuade decision makers to support their cause. The 1970s witnessed a strong commitment from national government to public participation, ushered in by several official reports published at the tail-end of the previous decade urging greater citizen involvement in the planning and delivery of public services (for example, Plowden, 1967; Seebohm, 1968; Redcliffe-Maud, 1969; Skeffington, 1969). Many community workers and activists saw this as an opportunity for marginalised people to find a voice, to articulate their concerns and to have some influence over decisions that affected their lives (for example, Barr, 1977; Symons, 1981). Community work was defined as having a fundamental role in promoting participation and increasing people's capacity to influence the decisions that affect them (ACW, 1978). For those with a radical analysis, removal of the economic and political barriers to participation constituted a core, but long-term goal of community development. Consequently, there was broad agreement that community work was concerned with social change and active citizenship, and that it had a primarily local dimension (Younghusband, 1968; Thomas, 1976). Influential community work 'texts' published around this time focused on the neighbourhood as the most appropriate level for community work interventions (Henderson and Thomas, 1980; Twelvetrees, 1982). During this period community development work was seen as localised and generic, having an overarching purpose of creating integrated and 'harmonious' communities, based on neighbourhood identity and a notional egalitarianism. The aims of the community worker were intertwined: on the one hand, to enhance a community's internal democracy by assisting local people in developing and managing their own organisations, and on the other, to enable the (preferably consensual) views of the community to be expressed to relevant decision-making bodies through representative leadership or participation in public consultation exercises.

Recognising and respecting differences

As Popple (1995) has observed, this 'golden age' in the late 1970s and early 1980s, with its relatively stable understanding of the main objectives of community work was soon to be shaken by the appearance of identity politics and separatist strategies for achieving social change. Drawing on the experiences of the women's and Black movements of earlier decades, community work was forced to engage with the debate around different dimensions of oppression (Mayo, 1977; Ohri and Manning, 1982). Marxist and feminist models of society were extended and challenged by the experiences and demands of gay men and lesbians, Disabled people and Black and minority ethnic communities. The different expectations and demands of older and younger people were also being increasingly acknowledged. Communities based on political identity or ethnic origin organised themselves separately, setting up parallel community projects and representative organisations. Within community development and the more radical parts of the voluntary sector, these strategies of resistance and emancipation were regarded as legitimate and necessary means of developing services and campaigns that asserted *specific* (sometimes competing) perspectives on a range of issues (Shukra, 1995). In more progressive local authority areas (mainly the Greater London Council and metropolitan boroughs), they received controversial recognition through grant-aid and political status on advisory forums or liaison committees. By constructing their own collective identity, 'communities of interest' achieved hitherto unknown levels of political influence. This was earned through contributing particular expertise and experience to decision-making processes while simultaneously attempting to shift the balance of power and resources within society.

A key political development over the past 20 years or so has been the growth of self-organised movements around different forms of discrimination and oppression. Alongside demands for equal rights and equal treatment has developed a recognition that this does not mean treating everybody the same, nor expecting people to conform to prevailing cultures or social expectations. There emerged a growing understanding that many people, perhaps the majority, experience multiple, interacting oppressions (Alperin, 1990) and steps are needed to meet people's practical and psychological requirements by working simultaneously with a range of self-organised communities. As a consequence of these struggles, a majority view gradually emerged within mainstream community work that anti-oppressive strategies and positive action measures should be incorporated into notions of 'good practice'. While this somewhat 'top-down' approach was contested in some quarters as being heavy-handed, 'politically correct' and ineffective, it did ensure that organisations were forced to consider issues around discrimination and access. By the 1990s equality had secured its position as a core value of community development. Funding for community-based projects became increasingly dependent on satisfactory equal opportunities policies and equality perspectives became a powerful driving force within community development, underpinning a strengthening commitment to participation and empowerment.

Achieving this demanded interaction between 'communities' on the basis of equality, tolerance and mutual learning (Sondhi, 1997). In this respect, community work has two contributions to make. The first is to provide the initial spans for building bridges across divides of prejudice and ignorance. The second role is more challenging and involves an acknowledgement that equality must be actively constructed, tackling power differentials, disagreements and downright hostility even when this confuses loyalties (Phillips, 1987; Modood, 1992). Models of anti-discriminatory practice have become incorporated into community work training and thinking. This involves working with those who are oppressed; developing confidence, esteem, skills and awareness. It also requires work with those who are either benefiting from the inequality (for example, through privileged access to resources or assumptions of normality) or actively defending it (Albrecht and Brewer, 1990; Gilchrist, 1992b; Thompson, 1998).

During the 1980s and 1990s the basis for community development shifted from long-term state funding of generic posts, such as neighbourhood development workers or community centre wardens, to relatively short-term project-oriented activities. Earlier, community workers had been able to articulate and respond to local issues as they became evident, helping residents to organise campaigns around, for example, the closure of a nursery, sources of pollution, or unwelcome planning decisions. However, these posts gradually disappeared in a welter of local authority budget cuts, with community and voluntary organisations being particularly hard hit. Between 1979 and 1997, under successive Conservative governments, community development practice became oriented more towards self-help training and service provision. Central government funding was available through a succession on Manpower Services Schemes for short-term initiatives designed to improve people's employability and encourage volunteering. The funding regimes of the 1990s meant that many community workers were employed on temporary contracts and had to concentrate their efforts on government priorities (homelessness, drugs, mental health and so on), by running community-based welfare services for specific 'client groups'.

Projects were required to set and meet targets, which were bureaucratically monitored and checked by external scrutineers. In the voluntary sector generic community development was largely replaced by issue-based work, carrying out government policies and tightly constrained by contracts or service agreements containing predetermined performance criteria and mechanistic auditing procedures (Gutch, 1992; Power, 1994). At the same time local authority community work became increasingly directive and less concerned with processes of education and empowerment. Instead, job descriptions tended to emphasise responsibility for grants administration, consultation exercises, service delivery, partnership arrangements and bidding procedures for regeneration funding (AMA, 1993). Consequently, work programmes were delivered and evaluated around much more rigid objectives, necessitating a greater degree of formal record keeping and accounting.

State-sponsored community work

The 1990s witnessed a gradual reduction in the role of statutory authorities in providing a range of welfare services. An alternative model of the 'enabling state' was proposed that saw local councils and health authorities as commissioning agents, contracting out public services such as home care, waste disposal, sports facilities and mental health support to the private and voluntary sectors. The intention was to identify efficiency savings and thereby reduce costs to the taxpayer. Many of these contracts went to commercial firms, but it was also an opportunity for voluntary organisations to develop a more stable funding base and to gain recognition for the valuable services they provided in the community. The drawback was the understandable requirement for greater accountability in service delivery and value for money, which restricted the critical and independent role of the sector. More nebulous activities that promoted community spirit and created community-based assets but did not lead to predictable (and measurable) outputs, were severely constrained or abandoned altogether. An early casualty was the provision of effective support for communities to develop their own ideas, skills and enthusiasm. The community worker's role in helping to organise community-led collective action all but disappeared, although campaigning itself did not, for example against the Poll Tax (Burns, 1992). The radicalism of earlier decades became muted and a new approach to working with communities was fashioned, termed 'community practice' (Butcher et al, 1993; Banks et al, 2003). Community practice refers to a relatively new kind of occupation, located usually within an institutional structure but with a remit for managing the interface between communities and statutory institutions, such as local government, the police or health agencies. Community practitioners are responsible for communication across this increasingly blurred boundary, and often play an important role in facilitating community participation in strategic decision making, for example through representation on local strategic partnerships or community planning exercises. Community practitioners might be responsible for outreach strategies, consultation exercises, partnership work and participation mechanisms such as neighbourhood forums and developing community leadership.

Increasingly, government programmes are managed through cross-sectoral partnership arrangements, with a requirement that the voluntary and community sector is represented not just by paid professionals, but through representatives from the target communities themselves. A plethora of area-based initiatives, often termed 'action zones', were established in the first few years of the New Labour government, attempting to improve health, educational attainment, economic regeneration, under-fives care, neighbourhood management and so on. Community involvement was seen as essential to their success and yet the people responsible for this new approach rarely had the skills or knowledge to engage effectively with the relevant communities, especially in the most disadvantaged areas. Government initiatives tended to focus on the role of individuals in communities, with funding schemes to support 'community champions', 'social entrepreneurs', neighbourhood wardens and the like. Capacity building was provided for individuals prepared to take up these roles, but there was little recognition that community leaders need mechanisms for support and accountability in order to carry out their role effectively.

Community members who did rise to the challenge became unfairly branded as 'usual suspects', and the pressure of partnership work often led to them becoming isolated and burnt out, or simply disillusioned by the whole process (Anastacio et al, 2000; Purdue et al, 2000). Similarly, initial attempts to 'consult with the community' were met with cynicism and 'apathy', often eliciting views only from a dominant minority or outright opposition.

There was a failure to understand that community participation requires a longer-term approach that:

- is sensitive to differences within communities;
- manages tensions and expectations; and
- includes a variety of ways for people to contribute their ideas.

Communities are not homogenous, rarely speak with one voice and are often sceptical about the intentions of local officials. The requirement for democratic representation is a challenge for even the most well-organised and articulate community. Those who have experienced years of deprivation feel deeply disenfranchised and angry. A necessary first step is to acknowledge these feelings and to help people to learn from their emotions and experience, channelling them into constructive and feasible strategies that can really transform the quality of life and open up new opportunities.

Regeneration and renewal

The revival of interest in community participation has been accompanied by an explicit commitment from government to promoting cohesion, diversity and social inclusion. The skills, values and understanding that exist within the community development field are vital to the success and sustainability of government programmes around economic regeneration and neighbourhood renewal. In particular, community development has much to offer in relation to strategies for:

- tackling social exclusion;
- increasing community involvement;
- building community capacity;
- promoting community cohesion;
- supporting social enterprise; and
- improving multi-agency working.

Community workers have become adept at working across many organisational cultures and social environments. This is important for developing cooperation across boundaries and for reaching out to sections of the community which are disaffected or appear difficult to work with for practical reasons. This focus on working with voluntary groups and marginalised communities acknowledges that these groups probably need additional support if they are to operate effectively within organisational environments dominated by powerful private and statutory interests. A key role for community workers is to provide and maintain communication channels between different sectors by linking different agencies and population groups. This is especially important where community representatives are involved. A recent survey of community work in the UK indicated that the number of such posts had increased since the 1990s but that these were often short-term, focused on specific tasks and managed by people with only limited understanding of community development (Glen et al, 2004). This situation makes it more difficult to build effective networks within the community and undermines the sustainability of such programmes. A networking approach needs a long-term perspective based on job security and relatively stable funding arrangements guaranteeing at least core costs.

An emerging profession

Community development is distinguished from social work and allied welfare professions through its commitment to collective ways of addressing problems. Community development helps community members to identify unmet needs, to undertake research on the problem and present possible solutions. Initially this may be on a self-help basis, pioneering different ways of addressing a particular issue. If this is successful and demand grows, the worker would assist group members to establish the initiative on a more secure footing, with a formal management committee, constitution, funding arrangements and paid staff. This transformation of a community-run activity into a voluntary organisation will be familiar to most community development workers but is not always a straightforward process. It will involve direct support of individuals as well as help with managing group dynamics and developing appropriate organisational structures. There may be times when the worker finds themselves in the role of advocate, occasionally even running the organisation, but mostly their function will be to support and guide community members, helping them to achieve their goals in the way that they have chosen. Community development is primarily concerned with meeting the needs and aspirations of community members whose circumstances have left them poorly provided for, often without adequate services, with limited means to organise and excluded from mainstream opportunities to participate in activities or decision making. Community development seeks to build collective capacity by improving skills, confidence and knowledge for individuals and the community as a whole. Community development also nurtures community infrastructure by supporting informal networks as well as formal organisations.

The Standing Conference for Community Development (recently re-named the Community Development Exchange), the umbrella body for community development in the UK, describes community development as being "about building active and sustainable communities based on social justice and mutual respect" (SCCD, 2001, p 5). The definition goes on to state that: "It is about changing power structures to remove the barriers that prevent people from

Table 1: Main values and commitments for community development

Values	Commitments
Social justice – enabling people to claim their human rights, meet their needs and have greater control over the decision-making processes which affect their lives	Challenging discrimination and oppressive practices within organisations, institutions and communities
Participation – facilitating democratic involvement by people in the issues that affect their lives based on full citizenship, autonomy and shared power, skills, knowledge and experience	Developing policy and practice that protects the environment
	Encouraging networking and connections between communities and organisations
Equality – challenging the attitudes of individuals and the practices of institutions and society that discriminate against and marginalise people	Ensuring access and choice for all groups and individuals within society
	Influencing policy and programmes from the perspective of communities
Learning – recognising the skills, knowledge and expertise that people contribute and develop by taking action to tackle social, economic, political and environmental problems	Prioritising the issues of concern to people experiencing poverty and social exclusion
	Promoting social change that is long-term and sustainable
	Reversing inequality and the imbalance of power relationships in society
Cooperation – working together to identify and implement action based on mutual respect of diverse cultures and contributions	Supporting community-led collective action

participating in the issues that affect their lives". This is accomplished by working with individuals, groups and organisations on the basis of the values and commitments shown in Table 1.

The Federation of Community Work Training Groups (a parallel organisation to SCCD and recently renamed as the Federation for Community Development Learning), has been working for some years on the national occupational standards for community development work and in a recently revised statement it identifies the key purpose of community development work as "collectively to bring about social change and justice, by working with communities to:

- identify needs, opportunities, rights and responsibilities,
- plan, organise and take action,
- evaluate the effectiveness and impact of the action, all in ways that challenge oppression and tackle inequalities" (FCWTGs, 2002, p 1).

Both these models describe the processes, skills and outcomes that are involved in community development work. In order to distinguish this from community activity or voluntary work, it is useful to think about the role that the community development worker plays in:

- *enabling* people to become involved by removing practical barriers to their participation;
- *encouraging* individuals to contribute to activities and decision making, and to keep going when things get difficult;
- *empowering* others by increasing their confidence and ability to influence decisions and take responsibility for their own actions;
- *educating* people by helping them to reflect on their own experience, to learn from others and through discussion;
- *equalising* situations so that people have the same access to opportunities, resources and facilities within communities and mainstream services;
- *evaluating* the impact of these interventions; and
- *engaging* with groups and organisations to increase community involvement in partnerships and other forms of public decision making.

These seven 'E's of community development make it clear that the community development worker is concerned not with their own interests and needs, but instead supports community members and activists to organise activities, take up issues and challenge unjust discrimination. Power is a dominant theme within community development, and in this respect, the role is fundamentally about working with people in communities so that they have more influence over decisions that affect them, whether this is about their own lives or about what happens in the world around them. Community development addresses and seeks to change relations of power within communities and society as a whole, and as such, it inevitably has a strong political dimension. However, this has usually become less about confrontation and more about compromise and negotiation, especially since the advent of partnership working.

Models of community development in the UK

Compared to law, medicine or even social work, community development is a relatively new profession. To some extent, it has become an instrument of state policy, designed to address perceived problems of what we now call 'social exclusion': poverty, discrimination and an apparent breakdown in public order. Community development has appeared under several auspices, including health, regeneration, crime reduction and so on, where there is shared belief that 'community participation' or 'citizen involvement' are necessary and desirable prerequisites for social improvement (Henderson, 2000; Taylor, 2000b). However, behind this apparent agreement lie three different models of community development, each related to contrasting political analyses of society and the state (see Table 2).

The first approach assumes that there is a broad *consensus* about social issues, how they can be tackled and how society in general should be organised. Within this model, state-sponsored community development projects have been devised to:

- encourage local responsibility for organising self-help activities;
- facilitate the delivery of welfare services, particularly to marginalised sections of the population; and
- support community ('user') involvement in 'democratic' processes of consultation and project management.

Community workers have been deployed to foster community spirit, for example through cultural activities, and to work with statutory agencies to ensure that services provided match local needs. The goal for this model of community development is social harmony through the provision of a welfare 'safety net' to those most in need, but with pressure to conform to prevalent norms of behaviour. Communitarian ideas around family and social responsibility underpin this approach, especially in relation to volunteering, parenting and active citizenship, as the embodiment of civil society, expressed through collective self-help and voluntary forms of association (Etzioni, 1993; Blunkett, 2001). Although communitarian approaches have found their advocates within community development, there have also been criticisms of its reliance on moral authoritarianism and its consequent failure to effectively understand and counter structural inequalities and power differentials (Henderson and Salmon, 1998).

The *pluralist or liberal* model contains a stronger sense that society consists of different interest groups and that these compete to influence decision making. This approach acknowledges that some sections of the population are disadvantaged in this struggle and community development is seen as enhancing public decision making by enabling them to be heard. The task of the community worker is to assist communities to organise themselves, to find a collective 'voice' and to put pressure on the policy makers to pay more attention to *their* needs. The pluralist model of community work is often found within local authorities in the job descriptions of neighbourhood workers or equalities officers, developing and supporting local or identity-based communities to participate in advisory forums and consultation exercises.

Table 2: Models of community development

Model	Political framework	Typical activities
Consensus	Conservative	Social planning
	Communitarianism	Self-help groups
		Volunteering
Pluralist	Liberal	Partnership working
	Social democratic	Advocacy work
		Lobbying
		Community capacity building
Conflict	Radical	Community organising
	Socialist	Campaigning

The more *radical* version of community development explicitly identifies *conflicts of interest* within society and aligns itself with the poor and other oppressed groups (for example, Baldock, 1977; Mayo, 1979; Cooke and Shaw, 1996; Ledwith, 1997). It argues that the causes of poverty and disadvantage are to be found in the economic system and reflect historical patterns of exploitation embedded in social and political institutions. It aims to reduce inequalities by addressing issues around discrimination and prejudice. Radical community work emphasises people's civil rights and strives for social justice, seeking to develop political consciousness and powerful forms of collective organising to effect social change through a redistribution of power and resources. At local levels, for example within communities and organisations, this might involve the development of 'anti-oppressive strategies' and helping people (individually and collectively) to challenge the roots of their disadvantage and to demand better or fairer treatment. Community workers using this approach see themselves as advocates and organisers, helping communities to organise themselves effectively to challenge the poverty and discrimination they experience.

Many current definitions of community work assert this model but it can prove more difficult to implement in practice, mainly because workers find themselves in situations where their best intentions are constrained by the expectations of employers and external funders. In reality, a community development worker or project might combine these models, adopting different approaches depending on circumstances.

Networking for community development

A key principle of community development is to ensure that participation in decision making is democratic and inclusive, enabling people to contribute as equal citizens and to learn through their involvement in such processes. Interaction with others is an inevitable and necessary aspect of this, and community workers have an important role to play in helping people to work together, to communicate effectively and to deal with the inescapable tensions and disagreements that arise from this work. Networks that connect individuals and different sections of the local community are an invaluable resource, functioning as communication systems and organisational mechanisms. The development of 'community' is about strengthening and extending networks of relationships between individuals, between organisations, and just as importantly, between different sectors and agencies. Working to establish and maintain these networks is fundamental to effective community development work.

The idea that the 'essence' of community is to be found among relationships, rather than within the physical environment of 'place' is not new. The early studies of 'community' were very much concerned with describing the interactions and connections among residents. Almost regardless of ideology or context, community development has been concerned with developing and negotiating relationships. In particular, some early women writers on the skills and methods of community work recognised the importance of contact making, communicating, convening and coordinating activities (Klein, 1973; Leissner, 1975), although the term networking appeared only in the early 1980s (Symons, 1981). From an early stage in the development of community work as a professional activity, writers and trainers have identified the role of helping people and organisations to cooperate and communicate across boundaries as a significant, perhaps unique, aspect of the job. A pamphlet published as part of the debate on community work roles and training described the job as a "general purpose facilitator of local initiative networks" (Griffiths, 1981, p 14) and Francis et al's (1984) survey of community work as an occupation concluded that the community workers themselves represented a "significant network of skills and commitment" (p 14). Liaison had already been identified as a key function in building multi-agency organisations such as "alliances, federations, standing conferences and more modest working groups at local level" (Thomas, 1983, p 159). He emphasised the linkages between people within neighbourhoods and the need to "strengthen", "renew" and "nurture" existing networks (Thomas, 1983, pp 171-3). These were seen as supporting political processes of sharing and dialogue. Fostering *informal* interpersonal and interorganisational linkages within communities requires particular expertise and a strategic approach.

Attitudes and relationships underpin organisational functions, such as communication and cooperation, especially in dealing with "some of the uncertainties and blurred boundaries which arise in community work" (Payne, 1982, p 133). Milofsky (1988a, p 7) wrote that "community development requires network-building" and Bell, in his evaluation of a community development project, refers to networks as "the crucial steps which take community work on the road to community development" (1992, p 32). Bell emphasised the need for unforced opportunities for people to meet and work together, building mutual recognition and confidence. He also saw community networks as creating "a new stratum in the power structure which offers the possibility for long-term and important change" (p 32). The debates around community work training in the early 1970s identified a role in fostering social cohesion through community activities and inter-organisational work. To do this, an understanding of local social systems and skills in informal communication and contact making was needed (ACW, 1975). In these early accounts the role of the community worker was described as discovering and utilising existing networks. Networks were regarded as something community workers needed to know about and could work with, but the idea of intervening to change or develop these configurations came later. A more proactive approach was gradually adopted that recognised that the formation and transformation of networks was a legitimate (and desirable) focus for professional interventions. In the second edition of their book on *Skills in neighbourhood work*, Henderson and Thomas devote an entire chapter to the skills and strategies of helping people to associate and maintain contact with one another, describing neighbourhood development as

> ... about putting people in touch with one another, and of promoting their membership in groups and networks.... In the act of bringing people together, neighbourhood workers are performing an essential role. (1987, p 15)

Within patch-based or community social work, there was a growing interest in networking across agencies and role boundaries (Barclay, 1982), a trend reinforced in the 1990s by care in the community and user involvement strategies (Beresford, 1993). Trevillion, an early proponent of networking for social care professions, argues that it promotes a 'culture' of community through

> ... activities which enable separate individuals, groups or organisations to join with one another in social networks which enhance communication and/or active co-operation and create new opportunities for choice and empowerment. (1992, p 4)

Thomas (1995, p 6) describes community development as "system maintenance", meaning the social processes and organisational development that had previously characterised community development. Community workers are expected to be in touch with a sometimes bewildering range of individuals and organisations. Their role in facilitating communication and cooperation within communities is alluded to in much of the early community work literature, in the guise of, for example, community newsletters, liaison meetings, tenants' federations, festivals, resource centres, social gatherings and forums that were often serviced, managed, or entirely run by community workers. These were, and remain, excellent vehicles for networking, enabling people to meet to share ideas and to gain experience in working together. As we shall see in later chapters, community workers often find themselves in key positions within formal and informal networks, coordinating the organisational arrangements as well as managing a complex array of interpersonal relationships.

Networking becomes a core competence

Since the 1990s networking has become increasingly recognised as an important aspect of community work (Gilchrist, 1995; Henderson and Thomas, 2002) and a necessary aspect of building partnerships generally (Geddes, 1998). Indeed, it is interesting that in the latest survey of community workers, networking has become the most commonly identified key role (Glen et al, 2004). The SCCD Strategic Framework recognises networking as a significant aspect of the work, arguing that it "depends on establishing and maintaining both organisational links and personal relationships" (p 20). The latest version of the framework for occupational standards for community development work, published in 2002 after extensive consultation, identifies "developing working relationships with communities and organisations" as a primary role and specifies "facilitating community groups and networks" as a core competence (FCWTGs, 2002, p 3). Many training courses and conferences now include sessions on networking practice that aim to make people more aware of how they can use and develop their networks.

What has not been so generally recognised is the more hidden work of assisting people to make connections and sustain relationships where there are cultural differences, practical obstacles or political opposition. This requires political awareness, emotional sensitivity and advanced interpersonal skills (Hastings, 1993, p 76) and can be a "slow and painstaking process" (Bassinet-Bourget, 1991, p 61). Community workers operate within complex multi-organisational environments so they need to be strategic in making links and building relationships among a huge variety of potential and actual collaborators, including people from all sections of the community. Community workers use themselves as a resource or a tool in this process, but do not usually have a 'stake' in what happens as a result of those connections. They act as guardians or custodians of the networks, rather than using them to promote their own interests. Responsibility for network development and management is increasingly recognised as a job in its own right.

Conclusions

This brief review indicates how, for over a century, communities have experienced the well-meaning intentions of community workers coming from different ideological positions and government programmes. Where it has been successful, community development has sought to strengthen connections between individuals, groups, agencies and sectors so that the needs and aspirations of communities can be effectively met through collective action and improved services. The work involved in establishing and maintaining these boundary-spanning linkages has come to be known as networking but has often been hidden from public view. The following chapters aim to make the skills and strategies that underpin networking more explicit and, hopefully, better recognised by managers and funders.

What is it about networks that they figure so prominently within the community and voluntary sectors? This question will be considered in the next two chapters, which explore specific features of networks as a form of organisation and their relationship with wider social environments, particularly looking at informal voluntary activity. Studies of the community sector and the emergence of community activities over time suggest that community groups, forums and semi-formal networks provide the seed-bed for the growth of more formal voluntary associations and campaigns (see Milofsky, 1987; Chanan, 1991; Elsdon, 1998). The networking approach to community development described in this book recognises the significance of informal networks in gathering the energy, motivation and resources needed to organise collective activities and address crucial issues around equality and social justice.

THREE

Network theory and analysis

How do you hold a hundred tons of water in the air with no visible means of support? You build a cloud. (Cole, 1984, p 38)

Introduction

In recent years the concept of networks as a form of organisation has gained in currency both as a metaphor and as an explanatory tool. The term seems to have been first used by Radcliffe-Brown in 1940 and early sociologists recognised its significance as an aspect of social living (Warner and Lunt, 1942). It offers a useful model for examining the interactions of daily life and thinking about community dynamics. Within community development, networks are increasingly seen as the means for coordinating collective action, supporting the activities of practitioners, and providing important means of communication through various technologies as well as face-to-face interaction.

This and the following chapter provide an introduction to network theory used to examine form and function. It reviews analytical models developed from group and organisational studies and identifies key features often associated with effective networking. Networks are presented as an effective mode of organising in complex, turbulent environments and play an important role in the development of successful coalitions and partnerships. Chapter Four focuses on networks as informal knowledge management systems and as mechanisms for supporting collective action in communities and social movements. A networking approach to empowerment is developed using a 'circuits of power' model that emphasises the value of boundary-spanning work in promoting cohesion and managing diversity.

The word 'network' can be applied to a whole variety of multi-agency configurations, but it is useful to begin by thinking about what distinguishes networks from other forms of organisation. An essential characteristic of networks is the web of lateral connections and avoidance of formal bureaucratic structures. As shown in Figure 1, a network comprises:

- a set of *nodes* (where connections are made either through individuals or organisational units), and
- the *linkages* between them (Wasserman and Faust, 1994).

Figure 1: Diagrammatic representation of a network

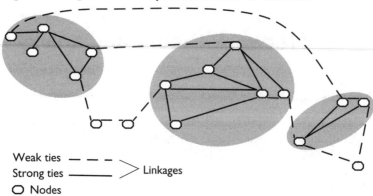

Weak ties — — — —
Strong ties ——————— > Linkages
○ Nodes

The significant thing about network ties is that they enable the nodes to influence one another, either directly or via the transfer of information.

In so far as networks have structure, they can be represented as polycentric and dynamic patterns of interaction, which are neither random, nor explicitly ordered. Networks operate on the basis of informal connections rather than formal roles, and membership tends to be voluntary and participative. The existence and vitality of the linkages are determined by personal choices, circumstance or occasionally sheer coincidence. Cooperation between members relies on persuasion and reciprocity rather than coercion or contracts. There are often no clear affiliation mechanisms (Ahrne, 1994), and membership itself is a fuzzy category with constantly shifting boundaries and allegiances. The tenuous nature of network connections makes it awkward to refer to network membership as if this were a defined category. Perhaps 'participant' is a more appropriate term, conveying the idea that networks are actively constructed and maintained, even though 'affiliation' may sometimes be unplanned or unwitting (Fineman and Gabriel, 1996). The most important and useful aspect of a network is its pattern of connections, which often reflects an underlying value basis, a shared interest or simply the geography of overlapping lives.

Broadly speaking, a network can be regarded as a complex system for processing and disseminating information. It is usually non-hierarchical with a range of access points and a multitude of transmission routes. This means that information can be obtained and sent between any number of different nodes without being monitored or censored. This is how the Internet operates and is a major factor in the resilience of networks to disruption or attempts to control the through-flow of information. Network-type structures are particularly useful in situations when information is ambiguous or risky, since contradictions can be clarified by turning to alternative sources for comparison and checking.

Dialogue and debate within networks transform information so that it becomes intelligence (about the current situation) and knowledge (about the wider context). This is vital for solving immediate problems and for adapting to a changing world. When Katz and Kahn (1966) compared three types of structure to investigate the optimal form for problem solving, they found that the 'wheel' model (all messages passing through spokes from hub to rim) was more suited to simple problems, than either a circle or a cross-connected web. However, as problems become more complex, then network models (with multiple lateral connections) come into their own, especially in situations of uncertainty (low or contradictory information) and constant change (Wilensky, 1967; Dawson, 1996). Such decentralised parallel-distributed processing systems are highly effective at managing ambiguous information and learning from experience. They are exactly the kind of organisational 'machine' needed to navigate the complex and turbulent landscape of human society (Scott, 1992; Mulgan, 1997). The psychologist, Donald Hebb, identified the neurological structure of the brain as the basis for human intelligence (1946) because complex neural networks have the capacity to coordinate action and to process information from a multitude of sources (Morgan, 1986; Bechtel and Abrahamsen, 1991). Community connections are like the axons and dendrites in the brain, integrating and transmitting information across linguistic and cultural boundaries like some kind of super-computer constantly revising a shared but dispersed model of the world (Dunbar, 1996).

Network analysis

Networks are neither groups nor organisations although they create the conditions for these to emerge. Networks enable members to form clusters that undertake specific activities, focused around a common goal or function, and coordinated on an autonomous basis. In the organisation literature this mode of organising is termed 'flexible specialisation' and is a feature of many complex systems, including, for example, those cutting-edge industries where innovation and creativity are at a premium (Sabel, 1989; Simmie, 1997). Early attempts to investigate the structure and function of networks originated in the Gestalt approach to human psychology, which recognised that in order to understand individual behaviour, it was necessary to study the 'whole' context, including interactions with others in the social landscape (Scott, 1991). Moreno (1934) developed the technique of 'sociograms' to map out the dynamics of small groups, while Lewin (1936) introduced the idea of the 'field' in which 'forces' shape social environments and influence individual behaviour, perceptions and attitudes. These initially crude mapping exercises drew on contemporary mathematical theory to build increasingly complicated diagrams that purported to represent enduring patterns of interaction. The resultant descriptions were thought to reveal significant features of social life.

Gestalt methods were applied to 'real life' situations and produced results that had the appearance of scientific rigour reinforced by an intuitive familiarity. Early studies of community relations carried out by the Chicago and Manchester schools of network sociology (for example, Park, 1925, 1929; Warner and Lunt, 1942; Mitchell, 1969) used both observation and interviews. The researchers noted patterns of interaction and also asked people about their personal affiliations. Rather than studying just individual actions, social network analysis (as it became known) was concerned with the array of informal relationships in order to understand the organisation or community as a whole. Deconstruction of the overall structure used the ties between people to map patterns of communication that could be used to identify, and even possibly predict, decision making and alliances (Laumann and Pappi, 1976).

Network analysis generated a number of useful theoretical developments in the social sciences, notably in sociology, anthropology and organisation theory. These include ideas around leadership, trust, decision making, coalitions and creativity, all of which are relevant to community development and social cohesion. Early network approaches to social behaviour explored the emergence of social clusters, such as acquaintance (Newcomb, 1961); friendship cliques (Boissevain, 1974); dissemination of rumours (Allport and Postman, 1947); the operation of prejudice (Allport, 1958); shifts in attitude and affinity (Homans, 1950); the management of conflict (Gluckmann, 1952) and the operation of power-blocs within democratic societies (Hunter, 1953; Miller, 1958). The social psychologist Milgram (1967) used the idea of interpersonal connections to explain the global reach of social networks in what has become known as the 'small-world effect', also popularised as the notion of 'six degrees of separation'.

Using a variety of analytical and presentation tools, network analysis provided a quantitative means of understanding the structure of social configurations and behaviour of individuals (Knoke and Kulinsky, 1982). Network researchers focused on the pattern and texture of the relationships in an attempt to explain how position in a network and the nature of the linkages affected social phenomena such as leadership, loyalty and identity (Gans, 1962; Webber, 1963). They looked at the nature and frequency of interactions: levels of intimacy, degree of reciprocity, and the strength of ties between individuals (for example, White, 1963; Kapferer, 1969). Of particular relevance is Granovetter's research on the strength of 'weak' ties. Granovetter (1973, 1974, 1978, 1985) investigated how people used personal connections to obtain information and share ideas. He identified the importance of the 'weak ties' between acquaintances and casual interactions in 'bridging' the gaps between different social clusters, and maintaining social cohesion in modern urban life. This was a useful counterbalance to earlier studies that had focused on networks based on the 'thick ties' of kinship and friendship operating within neighbourhoods and villages (Bott, 1957; Young and Willmott, 1957). Community development is mainly concerned with strengthening and extending the 'weak ties' or in social capital terms, the 'bridges' and 'links', particularly in situations where people find it difficult to meet and make connections. But bridges need support mechanisms, either in the form of sturdy structures at each end or a securely anchored suspension, especially when the ground is uneven or friable. Bonding capital of strong communities is crucial in supplying these foundations and also needs attention in the form of support to single-identity groups, for example, based on a common culture or origin (Butt, 2001). This is particularly relevant to strategies for building community cohesion in towns and cities that have been fragmented by ethnic, sectarian and other social divisions (Gilchrist, 2003c).

Several of the studies using techniques of network analysis generated some interesting observations regarding the operation of power in society (Knoke, 1990a, 1990b), and the importance of informal interactions within organisations (Emery and Trist, 1965). The methods of investigation were, however, fairly crude compared to the inherent complexities of most real networks and, unsurprisingly, network analysts tended to gather evidence in situations that were relatively stable, bounded and integrated. They largely failed to capture the intricacies and dynamics of personal relationships, especially where these involved tensions and negative attitudes. In recent years, network analysis has developed more sophisticated techniques of mathematical modelling that use computer programs to calculate statistical algorithms and display them in diagrammatic or matrix form (for example, Krackhardt, 1994; Stephenson, 1998; Freeman, 2000). Network analysis has found practical applications within organisation development and some welfare professions (Seed, 1990; Baker, 1994; Smith, 1996). It has not yet been used to evaluate the effectiveness of community development, mainly due to problems around data collection. Network analysis does offer a potentially fruitful avenue for community action research and participatory appraisal methods.

Organisational studies

Following the pioneering Hawthorne studies which looked at informal connections within the workplace (Mayo, 1960), organisation theory began increasingly to acknowledge the organic and psychological aspects of organisations that had hitherto been overshadowed by an emphasis on the impact of bureaucracy and technology (Burns and Stalker, 1961). Research into the structure and dynamics of organisations produced insights that are helpful in understanding the significance of networks in the coordination of social life (Thompson et al, 1991). Networks have been variously described as a new, intermediary, or hybrid form of organisation. Early organisation theorists believed that economic and social regulation takes place either through 'market' or 'hierarchical' mechanisms (Williamson, 1975). Ouchi (1980) was the first to propose a third form of organising that he termed the 'clan' or Z-model. Powell elaborated on this, describing networks as primarily based on relationships and reputation, describing a network as "an intricate lattice-work of collaborative ventures" (1990, p 269).

> In network modes of resource allocation, transactions occur neither through discrete exchanges nor by administrative fiat, but through networks of individuals engaged in reciprocal, preferential, mutually supportive actions.... [They] are especially useful for the exchange of commodities whose value is not easily measured. (Powell, 1990, pp 271-2)

The network model was originally proposed as a contrast to markets and hierarchies, but the majority of organisation theorists adopted a combined approach acknowledging that the three forms probably coexist within most organisations (Bradach and Eccles, 1989; Frances et al, 1991). Some considered networks to be an entirely novel form of organisation, suited to post-modern conditions (Cooper and Burrell, 1988), while others saw networks as encompassing all kinds of organisation (Baker, 1992), weaving a complex web of informal relationships in and around the formal structures. Colebatch and Lamour (1993) refer to networks as 'community' processes to distinguish them from bureaucratic and commercial transactions. True networks have no central organising or control mechanism. Function and authority is distributed across the nodes and linkages, such that decision making and implementation are conducted through informal and temporary coalitions of actors and resources. Within networks, influence operates predominantly through informal connections based on trust, loyalty, reciprocity, civility and sociability (Misztal, 2000). Network enthusiasts tend to emphasise their 'flatness' and flexibility, assuming network members enjoy a nominal equality and ignoring issues around elitism and exclusivity. In reality, networks also include relationships based on fear, jealousy, animosity and suspicion, all of which reflect patterns of power, "prejudice" and "personal" preference (Fineman, 1993).

Network or organisation?

Networks offer a mode of organising that brings about change by cooperation between autonomous and disparate bodies without formal procedures or structures. They enable resources and information to be shared and exchanged across boundaries without the necessity (or authority) of explicit contracts. Organisations, on the other hand, exercise control over jointly owned resources through protocols and explicit decisions. They function through roles and regulations that exist independently of who might be occupying or implementing these. In contrast, networks operate through connections between specific individuals whose attitudes and actions shape interpersonal interactions and incorporate local conventions. Organisations use rules to coordinate activity. Networks need relationships to influence behaviour and change minds. They are more flexible, less hierarchical and therefore more responsive to unexpected shifts in the environment. Networks live within and around organisations linking people in different departments and external bodies. Networks may well improve an organisation's performance, providing a hidden resilience and flexibility, but they can also sabotage an organisation's democratic structure and mission, undermining authority and circumventing official procedures.

These distinctions are summarised in Table 3, but are not always clear-cut. They provide a rough guide as to whether a network or an organisation is the most appropriate term to describe a conglomeration of people working together. This is not just a semantic issue, as we shall see later. Expectations are different for networks, and for some purposes these are not the most suitable mode of

Table 3: Key differences between networks and organisations

	Network	**Organisation**
Nature of connections	Interpersonal relationships	Formal procedures and lines of accountability
Membership	Fuzzy category, depends on on-going participation and interaction	Clearly defined by affiliation, subscription, employment
Nodes	Individuals/organisational unit	Roles/posts
Type of structure	Non-centralised web of connections	Usually hierarchical arrangement, with central control
Boundaries	Unclear, permeable; many boundary-spanning links	Defined and maintained, often through constitution or written protocols
Mode of interaction	Based on custom, personal history and mutual affinity	Rules and regulations
Basis of exchange	Trust and favours	Contracts and directives
Common bond	Shared values	Agreed aims and objectives

organising. Yet people often choose to set up loose networks when a more formal structure would do the job better and more democratically. Sometimes both types are needed and what starts life as a network has to transform itself into a formal organisation as its function and environment change. Community development is often concerned with developing organisations and working to challenge the policies of institutions. Understanding how networks operate is therefore vital to the work of community practitioners and managers (Gilchrist, 2003a). In particular, the routes through which information reaches people can crucially affect how new ideas are received in that we are more inclined to listen to and accept the opinions of those we know, like or admire. Similarly, it is important to recruit potential allies and helpers who will be supportive rather than block change or innovation.

A primary function of networks is to facilitate boundary-spanning cooperation, coordination and communication. They operate effectively in complex situations that are characterised by uncertainty, interdependence and opportunities for informal interaction across organisational borders. The value of lateral connections within and between organisations has been noted for some time. Decentralised networks, founded on norms and values (rather than administrative edicts) have an advantage over formal organisations in what Emery and Trist termed 'turbulent environments' (1965; Trist, 1983). By this they meant situations where there is rapid change and unpredictability. Benson (1975) took this one step further by introducing the idea of the 'interorganisational network' needed to cope with changing conditions by being more responsive, more connected and more creative. Informal patterns of interdependency among organisations have been identified as an important source of stability and coherence within complex fields (Perrow, 1979). In a network-type organisation, members are generally loosely connected through a variety of formal and informal linkages that enable them to share information or to trade with one another.

Firms in 'frontier' sections of industry, where innovation is at a premium, benefit from networking between their companies and in many regions have deliberately located themselves in clusters to maximise opportunities for the informal exchange of ideas (Hastings, 1993). Dynamic, personalised networks, which informally link separate firms or institutions create vital communication channels between organisations engaged in similar fields of research and development. These seem particularly important for supporting a rich intellectual environment that promotes learning and debate, appearing to benefit all concerned, at least during periods of growth (Kreiner and Schutz, 1990). It has been suggested that network configurations reduce transaction costs (Williamson, 1973), primarily through bonds of trust which are said to minimise risk and enhance mutual commitment (Perrow, 1992). But there *are* costs associated with networks, usually absorbed within informal (usually pleasant), social and quasi-professional activities. These costs accumulate outside the organisation's normal accounting procedures, through the invisible and un-audited trading of resources, ideas and favours. This has been demonstrated for the biotechnology and fashion industries (Simmie, 1997) and was probably true for older sectors such as lace-making, potteries and even computer software in their heyday. It is important to remember, in this respect, that it is the interactions and relationships that create the added-value, not simply co-location. There may be similar benefits for the voluntary and community sectors, where there are clear parallels in terms of stimulating change and pioneering new forms of provision, especially in the fields of education and welfare.

For several years within the voluntary and community sector the network form of organisation became the favoured alternative to hierarchy and competition, encapsulating (it was thought) egalitarian and democratic values often associated with the feminist and anarchist left (Ward, 1973; Ferguson, 1984). Somewhat paradoxically, and despite acknowledged examples of elitism and secrecy, many working on the radical wing of community development embraced the network model wholeheartedly. During the 1980s a host of 'network'-like organisations appeared to displace (in name at least) the federations, councils, associations and similar multi-agency conglomerations that had previously brought together diverse groups. Networks were assumed to operate according to principles of collective decision making and mutual accountability rather than bureaucratic control. They were not, however, the organisational panacea that many envisaged and often failed to fulfil their intended function. Networks have limited ability to reach and carry out consensual decisions and this makes it difficult to deal with internal disputes or conflicts of interest, resulting in hidden power elites which are difficult to challenge (Freeman, 1973; Landry et al, 1985).

Nevertheless, networks retained their presence, perhaps because the voluntary and community sector can itself be characterised as a turbulent environment, inhabited by interacting organisations that often compete for resources (members, funding, status). And yet informal relationships based on trust and shared values enable it to cooperate around matters of principle (Taylor and Hoggett, 1994; Paton, 1996). These interpersonal connections form a network of like-minded and dedicated individuals who serve on each other's management committees and are able to work together to coordinate activities and develop new organisations to meet emergent problems. The sector thus achieves both coherence and creativity without sacrificing the autonomy of separate organisations, or its ability to act in consort where necessary. However, many of the arrangements which support cooperation within the community and voluntary sector are "notoriously opaque ... whimsical and self-justifying" (Batsleer and Randall, 1992, p 199) and become disadvantageous when these positive links and affiliations prevent organisations from dealing with difficult situations, such as fraud, incompetence or discrimination. Improprieties and conflicts of interest may be deliberately hidden or simply underplayed in discussions in order to avoid explicit disagreements. This collusion is damaging and can seriously erode the credibility of the whole sector.

Partnerships and cross-sectoral working

The present fashion for partnership means that networking processes are even more necessary, and need to be adequately resourced. In the public sector, local government services have been gradually coaxed into complex area-based partnerships where cross-sectoral networks play an important role (Hambleton et al, 1995; NRU, 2002). The emphasis on 'joined-up' working, especially within government neighbourhood renewal and regeneration programmes, reflects two parallel concerns. They are seen as enabling coherent and efficient delivery of policy and services, and as a way of renewing local democracy by involving players from outside the state system in new forms of governance that sit alongside traditional forms of representative democracy. Issues around power, trust and accountability are key to understanding and improving partnership working. Partnerships formalise arrangements for joint venture through the sharing of resources and responsibility. Networks are often the precursors to these arrangements, and continue to be important in maintaining commitment, dealing with conflicts and ensuring proper representation. Effective networks enable information and resources to be shared across group and organisational boundaries. They provide the means to compare, challenge and contradict different versions of the world, and in doing so discover new ideas (Agranoff and McGuire, 2001). Strategies for managing diversity and promoting cohesion would benefit more than is generally realised from strengthening the boundary-spanning ties in order to improve informal relationships where there are differences and disagreements.

Trust is often mentioned as a key ingredient of such arrangements (Gambetta, 1988), although as Arrow (1974) (and Socrates before him) warns, trust is a 'delicate lubricant', an ephemeral and disarming virtue which can be evoked and revoked to suit the continuing power of professionals (Clegg and Hardy,

1996). In their study of community leadership, Purdue et al (2000) observed that feelings of trust and empowerment are linked, but that the power dynamics of the partnerships often obliged community representatives to trust the authorities because they had no sanctions and limited access to independent technical expertise. The legitimacy of community representatives is sometimes questioned when they challenge the prevailing assumptions and aims. This can lead to antagonism and withdrawal of cooperation from some partners. For communities to feel genuinely represented and empowered in these situations, they need to be able to trust their representatives, and to know that these in turn are trusted within the partnership structure. Networking contributes to this by building mutual commitment and generating trust. Without community networks supporting local leadership on these partnerships, state and market forces become much more significant in regulating social behaviour because the voices of users, residents or other potential partners/beneficiaries are distorted or suppressed altogether. In order to restore the credibility of community involvement it is necessary to build formal infrastructures (Stewart, 1998), as well as encouraging informal communication.

Face-to-face interactions that build trust are vital to both of these, and networking within and across the sectors provides an effective means of building new forms of accountability. Accountability issues arise whenever people are engaged in joint endeavours and permitted to act with discretion within a broad framework of agreed aims (Leat, 1988). This takes three forms:

• giving account – of what was done and why;
• taking into account – the interests of different stakeholders; and
• accounting for – the use of resources, especially finances.

In formal terms, accountability operates through systems of contracts, audits, scrutiny exercises and complaints procedures in ways that are usually transparent and quantifiable (Kumar, 1997). Alongside this, informal accountability is mediated through trust and integrity. Face-to-face interactions tend to increase 'felt' accountability (Burns, 1997), with a consequent bias towards familiar (and presumably liked) stakeholders. In this respect, informal networks constitute hidden and irregular policy communities, searching out opportunities to influence or subvert formal decisions (Jacobs, 1992; Laguerre, 1994). Voluntary organisations are particularly prone to these influences, tending to be accountable to several constituencies, including a range of funders and users. Without strong community networks holding leaders to account and providing them with support, there is a high risk of power corroding individual responsibilities and motives. Arrangements are needed that place a "premium on transparency and communication" in order to manage the multiplicity and diversity of expectations (Taylor, 1996, p 62).

Conclusions

An understanding of how networks operate within and between organisations is essential when it comes to helping communities to develop their own ideas and infrastructure. Many voluntary organisations and community groups evolve to meet a perceived need within communities. As we shall see in the next chapter, networks provide the conditions from which these initiatives spring. 'Well-connected' communities (with established voluntary associations and robust informal networking arrangements) are well-placed and well-equipped to make a major contribution to multi-agency developments around many issues and at all levels. Community workers, as individuals, often bear the hidden costs of networking through personal, 'out of hours' investment of time and emotion in relationships which benefit their paid work. This has become more significant in recent years with the increased demands on communities (often supported by community workers) to engage in inter-agency arrangements where boundary-spanning links are particularly helpful. Networks within communities, among people carrying out their normal, everyday activities, are also a vital source of social capital and community cohesion.

FOUR

Network functions

In life, the issue is not control, but dynamic inter-connectedness. (Jantsch, 1980, p 196)

Perhaps the most important, although somewhat tautological, function of networks is their capacity to support networking: enabling people to share ideas, consolidate relationships, exchange goods and services, and cooperate. Networks generally operate on the basis of shared values and informal connections that are maintained by a general reciprocal commitment. They differ from formal organisations in being less dependent on structure and tend to function through personal interaction between people who know (or know of) each other. For community development purposes, networks are important because they:

- provide robust and dispersed communication channels;
- create opportunities for reflection and learning;
- facilitate collective action;
- underpin multi-agency partnerships; and
- promote social cohesion.

Conversation and communication

A huge amount of information and 'common sense' is communicated via informal networks. Conversations among friends, acquaintances and neighbours convey rumour, opinion, local knowledge and news, allowing constant revisions to our understanding of the immediate and changing world in which we live. Networks can be used to suppress views that question prevailing assumptions and customs, but they are also the mechanisms by which subversive ideas circulate, gather momentum and finally surface to challenge the status quo (Laguerre, 1994). People use their informal networks to develop controversial or critical opinions, often initially through muted debates among known allies or conversations with strangers that allow them to reveal risky thoughts and arguments. The covert nature of these discussions allows alternative versions of the world to be constructed and for a new consciousness to emerge. Reflective conversation and 'critical dialogue' underpin several radical models of community development and informal learning (Smith, 1994; Cooke and Shaw, 1996; Ledwith, 1997). Freire's (1972) approach to emancipatory education uses a series of questions to expose the contradictions in social and economic systems, with a view to generating collective action to challenge these. This process of 'conscientisation' forms the basis for community work practice, which seek substantial social change (Popple, 1995). As Alinsky (1972) noted, "happenings become experiences when they are digested, when they are reflected upon, related to general patterns and synthesised". The fact that much of this occurs in settings where formal accountability and scrutiny are minimal or non-existent allows such conversations to be opportunities for exploring ambiguity, contradictions and dissent. Knowledge dispersed through networks does not become 'thinner' but rather provides a collective wisdom that is empowering because it creates a "people's praxis" based on direct experience and empathy (Rahman, 1993, p 80). Freirean methods of conscientisation use 'guided' reflection to examine received wisdom and build up alternative explanations for people's experience that (theoretically) enable them to change their situation (Hope and Timmell, 1984; Kirkwood and Kirkwood, 1989).

By talking together, comparing ideas, discussing common experiences, and perhaps undertaking some kind of joint activity, people come to understand and trust one another. It is this that lays the foundation for collective action. "Dialogue becomes a horizontal relationship of mutual trust. Trust is established by dialogue; it cannot exist unless the words of both parties coincide with their actions" (Freire, 1972, p 64). Informal networks are essential to processes of social change, especially those which open up access to new ideas or encourage incompatible views to be exposed through questioning and acknowledging differences (Humphries and Martin, 2000). This form of collective reflection encourages experimentation and the creation of new 'paradigms'. Networks allow for a construction of 'reality', which although subjective, is grounded in experience and able to generate new insights and solutions. Such exchanges can be liberating, leading to radical analyses and transformative action (Ledwith, 1997).

Not only do individuals acquire different ways of thinking about their own lives and the world around them, they are also able to learn skills, gain confidence and a sense of their own identity. The feedback and advice provided through personal networks allow people to form judgements about themselves in comparison with others and to keep track of their own reputations (Tolsdorf, 1976; Emler, 1994). Psychologists have found that people's sense of their collective identity is socially constructed within informal groups and networks (Tajfel, 1981; Abrams and Hogg, 1990). This sense of community or shared fate is an important ingredient in people's willingness to undertake collective action (Kelly and Breinlinger, 1996). Networks help to build relationships within and across communities, to span sector boundaries and to develop a consensus that can inform future strategies. A notion of the "common good" emerges based on a deeper wisdom derived from listening to, interpreting, comparing, reviewing and evaluating views from divergent sources (Barnett, 1994, p 183). As Bayley (1997) asserts:

> ... the most fundamental tenet of the community development approach is that the worker takes time to develop a real understanding of how things look from the standpoint of those with whom she is working, that is to understand the culture, the assumptions and the priorities of those she is seeking to help. (p 18)

These revelations form a shared understanding and 'collective intelligence' (Böhm, 1994). If knowledge is indeed power, then informal and collective learning represents a potentially important route to empowerment, because as Schön (1990) and others have observed, learning often involves 'unlearning' the older, perhaps more dominant ways of thinking. Discussion is a very important aspect of 'joined-up' working where organisations with quite different cultures and traditions are expected to collaborate around a set of objectives, often externally set. This takes time. Multi-agency organisations need common aims and priorities if they are to achieve their purposes. Informal networks often provide the spaces for 'behind the scenes' dialogue that ease tensions, enhance understanding and consolidate mutual commitment. The informality of these unrecorded conversations allow people to express their reservations, explore 'wild' suggestions and admit that they might be having problems with the 'bigger picture'. Within communities and organisations, social networks are used to seek clarification, obtain reassurance and build consensus, by providing a forum for "public talk" (Schuler, 1996, p 134) and a means of covert inquiry (Ayim, 1994).

Many forms of social and adult education acknowledge the importance of people learning from one another and this is viewed as a core process of community integration and empowerment (for example, Mayo and Thompson, 1995; Crowther et al, 1999). In his study of voluntary and community organisations, Elsdon (1995) highlights the learning that takes place across interorganisational networks, often through chance conversations, involving personal interaction. He stresses the importance of warm, caring, mutually supportive relationships that enable people to overcome barriers to learning and build their self-confidence. For many marginalised communities this is a necessary step along the road to collective action. Networks enable people to identify common concerns for themselves, and to articulate the issues that they want to pursue either through participation in a broad partnership arrangement or through self-organisation and campaigning.

Collective empowerment

Empowerment is achieved through learning *and* collective organising. It is a central principle of community development, and increasingly to be found in the rhetoric (if not the practice) of government initiatives around regeneration and renewal. The term has been used to refer to individuals, as in the various Charters (citizens', patients', passengers' and so on) of the 1990s that were essentially about consumer rights. More recent approaches have developed

'Compacts', setting out minimal standards for transactions and consultation between government and the voluntary sector. In this context, community development is primarily concerned with enhancing the skills, knowledge, confidence and organisational capacity within communities so that they can engage more effectively with decision-making bodies, such as local authorities and strategic partnerships. In recent years, it has begun to be acknowledged that empowerment processes require a redistribution of power, and therefore also involve changes in the culture and procedures of mainstream institutions so that these become more transparent, more responsive and less inclined to maintain control. Challenging powerful institutions and oppressive practices is a crucial aspect of community development, as is changing the flow of power through organisations and communities. Collective action is empowering in its own right because it enables people without much power to assert their interests and influence decision making. Networks contribute to empowerment on a psychological level, by enabling people to compare their experiences, learn from each other's successes and develop greater awareness of the wider politics of inequality and oppression. As we saw in Chapter Two, radical community workers have long been aware of the dispersed nature of power and have seen their central task as shifting the balance of power within society by helping people to make connections with others who share their oppression or predicament (for example, Alinsky, 1972; Baldock, 1977; Jelfs, 1982).

Empowerment is not as an 'all-or-nothing' strategy involving opposition and conflict. It can be considered as a continuous process of increasing capacity to influence decision making. The government's Policy Action Team on community self-help identified seven principles for community empowerment. These are:

1) Participatory democracy through local groups is complementary to representative democracy through local councils and should be treated as such.
2) Resource holders should strive to reach the most grass-roots level possible when disbursing resources.
3) The starting point for the development of a community should be the aspirations of that community not the plans of external agencies.
4) External agencies should welcome and respect, and not seek to circumscribe, the independence of community groups.
5) The proper balance between providing too little support and too much support will vary from time to time and place to place: it should be the subject of negotiation and agreement.
6) Clarity of relationships is crucial, with a recognition of obligation on both sides.
7) No one has all the answers: all parties should acknowledge that they can learn from all the others. (PAT 9, 1999, p 23)

A networking approach to community development seeks to increase influence primarily through processes of connection, negotiation and persuasion. In this model, empowerment occurs by reconfiguring relationships and patterns of influence, rather than 'seizing power'. Organisation development is an important strand of community development and community workers frequently find themselves assisting in the creation, management and occasionally dissolution of formal structures. Their work programmes are dominated by tasks relating to finances, constitutions, administration, legal responsibilities and public relations. What has been less recognised is the role played by community development workers in supporting and managing informal networks that are capable of promoting both autonomy and solidarity. Networks can be used for empowerment by mobilising a 'critical mass' of allies for achieving change, often using collective action strategies. Communities that have experienced long-term systematic discrimination often need assistance in setting up their own organisations, as well as positive action strategies to challenge existing power blocs (Christian, 1998). If power is distributed across shifting systems of relationships and stakeholders, rather than the political or legal establishment, then strategies for the empowerment of disadvantaged groups require more fluid and decentralised forms of organisation (Clutterbuck, 1994). By acknowledging the diversity of constituent elements, networks channel power to where it can influence decisions or affect the course of events, making things happen and exerting pressure towards (or against) different interests.

Social psychological models of social change (Schneiderman, 1988), organising (Hosking and Morley, 1991), collective action (Kelly and Breinlinger, 1996) and protest (Klandermans, 1997) demonstrate that empowerment and participation involve cognitive and emotional processes to discover or define a shared problem and develop a collective solution. Personal feelings and attitudes affect how people interact and their willingness to work together (Hoggett and Miller, 2000; Hustedde and King, 2002). The emotions that flow through community networks are an important dimension of organising that has too often been denigrated, but cannot be easily dismissed from real life (Fineman, 1993; Beres and Wilson, 1997; Wheeler, 1999). Emotions are a powerful basis for learning and motivation. Individuals use their personal networks to raise their esteem, awareness and aspirations. They nurture connections with people who can help them make the leap from victim to agent, thereby taking greater control over their own lives. Feelings of loyalty, admiration, love even, are often the driving force for many community and voluntary activities, but so too are the less positive emotions of pity, resentment, anger and fear, observed in the 'moral panics' that give rise to vigilante groups or campaigns against supposed local threats, for example, in relation to suspected pædophiles and asylum seekers.

Patterns of power

Within formal and informal arrangements it is impossible to ignore questions of relative power (Mayo and Taylor, 2001). In the early studies of organisation and decision-making, the issue of power was seen as relevant only in conflict situations where there are competing interests. The zero-sum model, as it came to be known, tended to assume that there exists a fixed amount of power and that this is distributed across actors (individuals or organisations) who exercise influence or authority *over* others in order to secure an intended outcome or promote a particular interest (Weber, 1947). Imbalances of power ensured that certain interests prevailed, even in the face of explicit opposition or resistance. The capacity to organise, to 'mobilise bias' in one's favour, was identified as a crucial aspect of this 'first face' of power (Schattschneider, 1960; Dahl, 1961). But power also appeared to operate in the absence of overt conflict and without the use of force or sanctions. Power can also be exerted more surreptitiously than the above model of powerful and self-interested leadership indicates. Bachrach and Baratz (1962) suggested that this 'second face' of power operates by suppressing controversy and restricting opportunities to challenge prevailing norms and institutions. Thus contentious issues are suppressed, dissenting views are excluded from discussion and conflict is safely averted.

Radical political theorists have identified an additional form of power, which is even more pernicious. Lukes (1974) extended the debate around power by introducing a 'third dimension' which infiltrates the hearts and minds of 'ordinary' people to induce attitudes and practices which protect the interests of the elite or governing class. In many respects this is akin to Gramsci's (1971) earlier notion of 'hegemony', whereby 'common sense' and 'internalised oppression' are reproduced through cultural and civic institutions (Cammett, 1967). Both these formulations emphasise the power of indoctrination as opposed to authority exercised through control or coercion. Their approach suggests a model of power that is more diffuse and less attached to particular 'agents' or objective interests. It recognises the possibility of mutual influence and resistance through the development of countervailing ideas and social forces, or as Gramsci proposed, the construction of an alternative position or 'counter-hegemony' (1971).

Empowerment usually involves shifts in power relations *within* the system, but networks are not by definition empowering or progressive. Early studies of community power found that the pattern and quality of connections across social networks are major factors in being able to promote or protect particular interests (Hunter, 1953; Dahl, 1961; Hampton, 1970). Knoke's studies of public decision making (1990a, 1990b; Knoke and Kulinski, 1982) explicitly focused on the power of persuasion and the flow of opinion through personal and structural linkages. A prominent and reachable position in the network endows the occupant with disproportionate influence over fellow decision makers. This allows them to preserve privilege or exert unwarranted power. The secretive nature and concealed deliberations of friendship clusters render them unaccountable and exclusive (Freeman, 1973; Newman and Geddes, 2001). Networks can be cliquey and elitist, enrolling members through bizarre systems of preferment and ritual, such as experienced by apprentice freemasons. The 'old boy' network, based on public schools and Oxbridge colleges is said to exert a strong and enduring influence on opinion formers within British politics. Miliband (1969) demonstrated how the social networks of the upper classes were woven into the British state and recent commentaries by Paxman (1990) and Hutton (1995) confirm that little has changed in the intervening years despite the supposed advent of equal opportunities procedures in public recruitment and selection.

Nevertheless, networks provide the foundation and 'life-blood' for a variety of multi-agency organisations, ranging from formal consortia with specific remits set out in a constitution or memorandum, through open forums, to the most flexible of informal alliances. All of these are important vehicles for developing collective action and are often based more on faith and trust than explicit rules. At a collective level, networks help people to find allies and build organisations to promote their views within and outside the decision-making arena. This can be used to develop internal problem-solving strategies or to assert a particular viewpoint. Networks often underpin techniques for self-organisation among populations which are scattered, isolated or oppressed. Political activists will be familiar with the use of caucusing to influence and mobilise others to support a particular position or faction. Community development uses similar, but more open, methods of coalition building to challenge vested interests and empower communities.

Power has elastic, effervescent qualities (Maffesoli, 1996). It can be facilitative and generative: a vital force for achieving cooperation and mutual benefit rather than dominance and exploitation. Social networks channel power for collective ends by maintaining solidarity and allowing risk to be shared. Women theorists in particular have asserted the positive aspects of power as a productive and enabling resource (for example, Elworthy, 1996). They have stressed the importance of building facilitative connections in order to initiate and manage organisational change (Kanter, 1983; Helgesen, 1990). Wheatley (1992, p 39) regards power as the "capacity generated by relationships" which she sees as energy flowing through organisations, facilitated rather than controlled by those in positions of leadership. As Florence, a rural health trainer in South Africa, recognised:

> I have learned not to under-estimate the strength of each woman, organisation and community.... Every woman is born with that power, it is not created by the [Western Cape] Network, but the Network enables women to use their power. (Womankind Worldwide, 2000, p 6)

Postmodernists have likewise emphasised the dispersed and dynamic nature of power (Foucault, 1977, 1980; Bauman, 1991). They focus on the micro-practices governing relations between people, and between people and institutions, arguing that power differentials within systems direct the flow of influence towards and against decisions. Postmodernism regards power as fluid, inherently ambiguous and multifaceted (Hindess, 1996). It affects the patterns of interaction in everyday life, influencing behaviour and thinking without recourse to explicit force or actual punishment. Power relations are embedded in organisational cultures and personal behaviour to the extent that different dimensions of oppression become internalised in our personal and collective identities (Digeser, 1992). Alternatively, the flow of information and commitment through networks generates synergy and can be seen as empowering, especially for those who have been excluded from or deprived of opportunities to participate in decision making or collective activity.

This articulation of power as flowing through a network of relationships has been further developed by Clegg (1989, 1994) in his 'circuits of power' model. Clegg argues for "the centrality of processes of power to organisation, and of organisation to the processes of power" (1989, p 20). A networking approach to empowerment adopts a similar model of power, recognising that it can be positive, contextual and relational (Dawson, 1996; Servian, 1996). Agency, the capacity to make things happen, is achieved by making connections so that power can flow to where it is most effective. In recent years, community work appears to have adopted, perhaps unwittingly, this postmodern approach to empowerment. In a network model:

> The reality is that power does not reside in any one place. It is dispersed and the system of power can be activated anywhere. The important thing is to find ways of exerting leverage in the system.... Perhaps the really important thing is to realise that you have the power to change yourself, your way of thinking about power, your way of working with power. Once you do that, you are changing the way people will respond to you. (Gaffney, 1996, p 68)

This approach (which is fairly typical of recent community development thinking) reiterates a long-standing emphasis on process and personal empowerment (cf Biddle, 1968). Although community workers must avoid abusing the power of their professional role, they will inevitably apply their knowledge and skills to influence the opinions and behaviour of community members, and use their status and connections to change the policies and practices of institutions. As Shuftan explains, "empowerment is not an outcome of a single event; it is a continuous process that enables people to understand, upgrade and use their capacity to better control and gain power over their own lives" (1996, p 260).

At one level, it could be said that it is factors in the social environment that empower (and oppress). Processes of empowerment might include increasing, improving and incorporating useful and positive connections into the routine interactions and habits of people's everyday lives. Rees (1991) recognises the importance of networking practices within empowerment strategies, especially where these enhance credibility and influence for communities within decision-making arenas and encourage creative thinking. Empowerment is about self-help *and* collective organising. For the individual, networking is self-empowering (Cheater, 1999) because it reduces isolation, provides supportive mentoring and offers personal advancement. Self-empowerment is crucial to the achievement of collective goals and involves individual shifts in consciousness and confidence as well as campaigning. This was recognised by the anti-slavery campaigner Frederick Douglass, who declared that "If there is no struggle, there is no progress ... power concedes nothing without a demand. It never did and it never will" (Douglass, 1857). Almost by definition, empowerment is anti-oppressive because it involves challenging discrimination, prejudice and marginalisation (Mullender and Ward, 1991).

This has important implications for how community development workers operate to promote and maintain community networks, making sure that the power of leaders and representatives (including themselves) is both earned and accountable. The 'circuits of power' metaphor helps us to see empowerment as altering the flow of power through connected series of events and decisions, often operating through parallel relationships (cf Gilchrist and Taylor, 1997). Networks re-connect people and power and provide an important part of a community's capacity to secure viable and sustainable regeneration strategies (Taylor, 1998). By opening up experiences of oppression, exploitation and injustice to shared scrutiny, community networks encourage mutual responsibility and a solidarity that "recognises that people are not just individuals, that there *is* such a thing as society" (Jacobs, 1995, p 21).

The complex nature of power – its association with protecting elites as much as with promoting solidarity – presents networking strategies for community development with a dilemma. Networks are complex and dynamic. Unlike organisations, they cannot be controlled or moulded to a particular purpose. The connections grow and wither away according to their usefulness, rather like routes across a natural landscape (Finnegan, 1989). In this sense, community workers operate as social engineers, using relationships and interorganisational links to carve out new channels, construct pathways, clear away the undergrowth, erect bridges and occasionally tunnel into the depths of seemingly impenetrable institutions. Working to alter the flow of influence and information through these informal networks opens up access to resources and contributes to a redistribution of power.

Alliances for social change

Networks help people to learn from their experience, to articulate personal problems as shared issues and to organise for collective action. Research on social movements reveal that networks are informally maintained and continue to exert influence on policy formation and the emergence of temporary coalitions, even when they appear to be dormant (Rupp and Taylor, 1987; Morris, 1992; Melucci, 1996). Communities are the 'incubators' of collective activity with social networks acting as 'mobilising devices' (Tarrow, 1994, pp 21, 136). It is often useful to cultivate links beyond the immediate community, building alliances with individuals and organisations that have greater access to power and resources. Formal organisations are important but they are not the only means of collective empowerment. Models of the 'new' social movements have consistently stressed their fluid, diverse and organic nature (Lowe, 1986; Scott, A., 1990). In contrast to more traditional social movements (such as the trades unions or early tenants' organisations), they might be described as networks of networks in that they are more flexible, avoid central control mechanisms and seem content to operate with high levels of autonomy and low formal accountability. In recent years, social movement theories have begun to recognise the crucial role of informal networks in developing and sustaining involvement in mass political activity (Castells, 1997; Klandermans, 1997). There is a growing recognition of the micro-social processes of collective action: the interactions, the dialogue and the emotional ties between participants. The alliances that emerge need to be flexible and robust so that they can accommodate the diversity of experience and values that motivate people. This broadness of spirit and the colourful 'rainbow' image of such coalitions provide a model for collective organising that values diversity, promotes solidarity *and* supports challenging interactions (Bunch, 1990; Phillips, 1994).

Coalitions represent temporary, tactical arrangements through which disparate actors combine forces in order to achieve a goal that benefits each of them or fends off an external threat. They are generally semi-formal, ad hoc arrangements whereby separate agencies coordinate their activities in order to share resources and operate better in an uncertain environment (W.R. Scott, 1992, p 201). As Boissevain (1974) asserted, coalitions tend to emerge from networks of 'friends of friends', including the tangle of loose associations that characterise neighbourhoods or interest communities. A coalition might be built in response to events, forming a pragmatic and informal 'action-set'. Its aims will generally be focused on achieving a limited goal, such as winning a policy decision, organising an event, defending or obtaining a common resource. Once the coalition has achieved its purpose it may either dissolve or transform itself into a more structured organisation that could take on the management of a service, a building or other more permanent project. Networks may themselves become organisations, through formalising constitutions, or they might spawn new organisations, creating structure for specific purposes while leaving the networking function intact. The transition to more formal structures is neither always universally desired nor even feasible. Difficulties often arise where there is resistance or lack of clarity as to why a network needs to encumber itself with the constitutional trappings and formal accountabilities of a 'proper' organisation.

Developing community action

It is well known within community development that people tend to become involved in community activities or to join a local organisation if they already know someone involved or are persuaded through personal contact with a community worker. It takes a lot of courage or sheer desperation for someone to come along to an event without a prior introduction or conversation. A poster announcement or leaflet invitation is rarely sufficient, while information provided via websites is usually too remote and impersonal to support sustained participation. Generally, people enter into collective arrangements because they are already linked in some way with others involved. A connection exists which persuades them that the benefits of engagement are likely to outweigh the costs. The element of risk can be countered or dispersed through judicious networking to identify reliable allies and reach a modicum of consensus. The networking approach to community development helps people to develop useful relationships and find a common cause. In addition to psychological factors, local norms and conventions seem to play an important role in creating the conditions for effective collective action (Hardin, 1982; Chanan, 1991, 1992).

Social networks act as communication channels, encourage a sense of shared purpose (Melucci, 1989; Morris, 1992; McClurg Mueller, 1994) and are used to recruit for community-based organisations (Milofsky, 1987). Networks supply cost-effective means of achieving a 'critical mass' of support, which encourages wider participation. Four key factors appear to influence people's readiness to contribute to a collective initiative:

- the motivation of potential participants;
- the availability of resources;
- ease of communication; and
- social processes of interaction.

Marwell and Oliver (1993) suggest that in the initial stages of developing collective activities, organisers use their social ties to contact people who are most likely to participate, ensuring that a threshold for collective action is achieved as soon as possible. Organisers with many 'weak' ties in their networks are able to target, canvass and recruit potential contributors across many organisations and social groups. These boundary-spanning links are relatively cheap forms of communication, but highly effective in contacting sympathetic allies and mobilising resources. Knowledge about the interdependencies and connections among the network members is vital in making good use of the network as a communications system, otherwise the flow of information might be disrupted by channels that have deteriorated or become dysfunctional because people have fallen out or lost touch with one another. Effective organising requires a balance between the costs of maintaining networks (time, effort, money or other resources) and the expected gains. Each individual makes their own decision about how they can contribute, but this is influenced by the perceived decisions and behaviour of those around them.

Box. 1: Networking for the Bristol Festival Against Racism

In the initial stages of organising the 1994 Bristol Festival Against Racism the coordinator used various networks to distribute information about the proposal. Flyers were included in the mailings of several city-wide umbrella bodies, and announcements inserted in the newsletters of others. They were chosen because the organisers already had contacts in these organisations and anticipated that members of these organisations would be favourably disposed towards the idea. In addition, a number of key individuals were 'targeted' to persuade them to endorse the project, knowing that this would encourage others to come on board. Where there were gaps in the network, the coordinator made use of personal connections to identify a point of access, for example to the Travellers' community. Every opportunity was found to talk about the Festival and to make sure that the flyers reached the less obvious and less accessible nooks and crannies of Bristol's population. Once the initiative had gained a certain status and momentum, the local media also became interested and publicised the idea to an even wider audience. Thus, from a relatively small, but crucial set of links, the Festival became a major event, galvanising many people to contribute in some way and to take part in an explicitly anti-racist activity, often within their own community.

Marwell and Oliver (1993) emphasise the role of 'entrepreneurs', who may come from outside the community of interest and disproportionately absorb the costs of organising, perhaps for political or moral reasons. These individuals often have useful resources and skills to offer and can act as brokers or catalysts to get things started. They tend to be well connected with other resourceful or influential people. In this respect, it would appear that extensive and diverse networks are more advantageous than overlapping, close-knit sets of similar people bound by strong ties and shared outlooks. Individuals who are linked, but slightly peripheral to several distinct networks are more likely to provide the 'bridging mechanisms' that allow for cross-fertilisation of ideas and create the conditions for creative thinking. This is often the role played by community workers and community leaders, and can prove problematic for those individuals in situations where there are many tensions and differences.

Community cohesion

Working within and between diverse communities in ways that simultaneously honour different cultures and challenge inequalities can be a complicated process. The concept of community should be able to encompass and express both variety and unity (Murdoch and Day, 1995). A commitment to dialogue and working with the dissonances that arise can be expressed through formal coalitions, ad hoc alliances or informal networking. Networks work to accommodate divergence and dissent, rather than attempting to impose either unity in action or a spurious (and often fragile) consensus. Networks are particularly adept at managing change and contradiction, and are useful organisational tools for promoting genuine understanding and integration. Tolerance and transparency will be key principles in ensuring that power, intelligence and ownership are distributed across all stakeholders (Mulgan, 1997). This is true for organisations as well as individuals. Diversity challenges dogma and orthodoxy by generating alternatives. It allows a flexible response to uncertain conditions and this is important for the voluntary sector as well as social integration at community level (Forrest and Kearns, 2001).

Networks offer a means of stabilising 'turbulent' environments (Scott, R., 1992) and dealing with intercommunal tensions. Conflicts often arise because people want to use communal space for apparently incompatible purposes. Antagonisms appear, for example, because of differences in age, culture, gender and sexual orientation. Informal networks can be used to foster a "democratic and permissive culture" in communities and organisation, creating "the capacity to contain conflicts without being exploded apart by them" (Jeffers et al, 1996, p 123). Boundaries are transformed into borders that can be crossed by treating "difference and commonality not as static opposites" but as dimensions of interaction that can be shaped through the politics of love, trust and dialogue (Nelson et al, 2000, p 356). Community workers frequently operate in situations characterised by conflict and resistance, especially when they are helping communities to challenge poverty and discrimination. The 'outsider' can contribute by coordinating and facilitating such interactions, acting as a 'weak' tie, helping people to communicate directly, and interpreting when things get awkward. Pindar's (1994) study of a community's response to racial harassment refers to the role of an external 'champion' to propel and support inter-agency networking, thus ensuring that the core group was representative and democratic.

Policy initiatives to promote community cohesion have mainly been concerned with issues around fragmentation and the need to build cross-community contact, rather than addressing deep-rooted racial prejudice and inequality. Consequently, strategies for promoting community cohesion tend to assert the need for unity based on the integration of different cultures and experiences within society. Recent guidance defines a cohesive community as "one where:

- there is a common vision and sense of belonging for all communities,
- the diversity of people's different backgrounds and circumstances are appreciated and positively valued,
- those from different backgrounds have similar life opportunities, and
- strong and positive relationships are being developed between people from different backgrounds in the workplaces, within schools and within neighbourhoods" (LGA, 2002, p 6).

Networks can help to anticipate and diffuse tensions before they become full conflicts. By tackling ignorance, dogma and prejudice, a foundation of understanding and empathy can be established for analysing and dealing with differences. The relative informality of networks enables contrasting cultures and perspectives to be explored without them necessarily becoming confrontational, and where there *is* opposition, positive experiences of working together, of finding consensus in the past, make it more likely that solutions or compromises can be negotiated (Gilchrist, 1998a). Cross-cutting area-based forums provide opportunities to build bridging and linking social capital, creating relationships between people from different backgrounds and with different remits. Inequalities in power and access must, however, be addressed if such opportunities are not simply to become occasions for further disempowerment of community members, especially those from already marginalised groups. Community work posts are often located at the margins of organisations and have a special concern with boundaries and barriers (Williams, 2002). Vital and difficult work takes place across interfaces, between partners, and between different sections of the community. Community development values and methods are important in managing the overall web of connections to promote empowerment and support participation. The primary function of the professional community worker is to establish and nurture the 'bridging capital' to be found among the 'weak ties' of community and interorganisational networks. Networks build relationships that connect people who might otherwise find neither reason nor means to interact. The patterns of power within networks inevitably reflect the social and economic environment, and community workers have a key responsibility in making sure that the flow of resources and influence through networks is as egalitarian and democratic as possible.

Conclusions

The evidence presented in this and the previous chapter has indicated just how important networks are in our daily lives and in regulating society as a whole. They seem such a natural part of life that it would be easy to imagine that networks just happen without any particular effort or thought. However, a few minutes reflection on how we sustain and shape our own networks reveals that time and attention is needed to keep certain links intact, and we probably invest more in those connections that are useful or bring pleasure. Life events, such as births, marriage and death, are important occasions for reinforcing family ties and expressing our commitment to friends. Cultural or religious celebrations present opportunities for initiating or at least maintaining friendly relations with colleagues, neighbours and members of our community through the exchange of greetings and gifts, often accompanied by updates on personal news. The activities that are used to do this can be grouped under the generic term of networking, which will be the focus of the next two chapters.

FIVE

The principles and processes of networking

To understand is, as ever, to put choice in place of chance. (Charles Handy, 1988, p 113)

Introduction

Networking involves the creation, maintenance and use of links and relationships between individuals and/or organisations. Networking itself is a neutral tool – it can be used for a variety of purposes – selfish, political, altruistic or simply to get things done. Networking for community development is obviously influenced by key values around equality, empowerment and participation. Networking is increasingly seen as a popular, albeit mildly manipulative, means of gaining personal and political advancement. There is even a *feng shui* guide on how to attract (and presumably retain) influential people into one's personal networks (Too, 1997). This chapter looks at networking as something that most people do in their everyday lives, namely develop and maintain links with a selection of the people they encounter in their work, where they live or in the course of social or leisure activities. Since this book is about community development, it is not primarily concerned with the relationships that constitute our family and friendship networks, although of course there is some overlap (Pahl, 2000). The focus is rather on connections with colleagues, neighbours and the people we know through a variety of activities and who we regard as members of our different communities. Some of these may be no more than familiar faces; others might be nodding acquaintances, others may be people we chat to while out and about, or at a club, but who we would not necessarily invite to our homes. Others again we may know because of their role in an organisation that is significant in our lives.

Relationships constitute more than mere contacts or connections. They have an emotional content, sustaining people in their jobs and enabling them to undertake specific tasks by providing access to vital resources, knowledge and influence, which might not otherwise be available. In order to be effective, these relationships need to be authentic, reliable and holistic. They do not require intimacy, merely trust and respect. Interpersonal relationships within the community and between organisations need to be given greater credence within community development to ensure that they are established and maintained in ways that contribute to the overall work programme of individual workers or agencies. The networking approach advocated here requires that community workers have a good understanding of how relationships function and how they can be sustained. Community workers facilitate these processes by finding connections, creating opportunities for shared activities and encouraging dialogue across apparent boundaries.

The evidence used in this and the following chapters was mainly gathered from a case study of the coordination of the Bristol Festival Against Racism and a panel study involving 11 community development workers, asking them about their involvement in networks and getting them to reflect on their own experience of networking to identify how this contributed to their work and what made them 'good' networkers (for details of research methodology, see Gilchrist, 2001). Here we use findings from the panel study to examine successive phases of developing a relationship, from contact, through consolidation to maintenance. We look at key aspects of networking that are relevant to relationship formation, including modes of communication, building trust and managing diversity. The chapter considers how we use those connections to:

- give and receive support;
- obtain and share resources;
- influence the behaviour and attitudes of those around us; and
- anticipate and deal with conflicts.

What makes a good networker?

A theme that runs throughout this book is the strategic nature of networking. Like other aspects of community development it involves planning and evaluation. Preliminary research and preparation might be undertaken even before the initial contact, for example, making a conscious decision about whether to attend particular events on the basis of the participants list. Members of the research panel reported that they scanned these lists to target useful contacts and used their knowledge to decide where to sit or which workshops to go to. They would also think about how to present themselves (protocol, dress codes, use of jargon) and generally how to manage that first impression. Clearly this needs sensitive judgements about other people's expectations or about what circumstances dictate as 'appropriate' behaviour or language. Non-verbal communication provides important clues about other people's intentions and emotions (Eibl-Eibesfeldt, 1989; Zabrowitz, 1990). Community workers described how an unknown colleague at a conference might be approached because they 'looked interesting', held a certain position or behaved in a particular way that caught their attention, such as laughing at something that had been said or making eye contact. The ensuing conversation fulfils at least three simultaneous functions: to establish rapport, to gain information about the other and to impart information about oneself. The interaction can be fairly informal and often takes place in a social setting, such as during a refreshment break or while travelling. Networking exploits opportunities that are incidental to, but a necessary adjunct to, the 'main event'. Such interactions can be used to seek out common connections, and may involve a far-ranging series of conversational leads, including disclosure of personal matters.

> "What I tend to do is try and ask about the person, try and find out a bit about them and ask about their work or find something to talk about which perhaps isn't related to work, find some sort of common point that we could talk about." (TD)

The panelists felt that they generally adopted an informal style, without being or appearing casual. They engaged people in conversations around their likely interests, pitching and moderating their language accordingly, and used humour to put people at ease or when expressing a slightly ambivalent or unorthodox position. There was a strong sense that sustainable networking needed to involve convivial experiences, since most such interactions would be voluntary.

Panelists identified interpersonal skills as important and considered themselves as highly proficient in one-to-one interactions (where they referred to counselling-type techniques, such as listening and clarifying), as well as in group situations. Good networking involves accurate interpretations of individual conduct and group dynamics. It sometimes means intervening in situations to shape or open up interactions that are being distorted or blocked for one reason or another. Some of the relationships maintained might not be consciously selected, but develop anyway through reciprocal attention and care. Panelists made sure that they stayed in touch with certain colleagues at a personal level, even where contact was predominantly work-related. This included 'phone calls, making time in conversations to share personal news and views, marking significant life events and generally arranging social time together.

> "I would offer help and support, would sort of make some space to have a bit of a personal chat as well as a kind of work chat, so like 'How are you? How's life? How's bla bla bla?' and then 'oh well then so what's this about?', or at the end of the conversation after we dealt with the business, you sort of say 'well, how are things going for you then?'." (FB)

What seemed to characterise people's aptitude for networking was not so much specific tactics, but the versatility with which people were able to use them to develop their connections with a *wide range* of people. Networking requires an ability to operate appropriately in different organisational and cultural settings using the balance and adaptive capacities of a chameleon (Trevillion, 1992). Good networkers need to be able to interpret and transmit information across boundaries, directing it in appropriate formats to where it might be useful. Flexibility and informality appear to be significant qualities, an important point for people accustomed to working in bureaucratic environments (Kickert et al, 1997). It is important to come across as confident in unstructured social settings, but to be aware that not everyone present would feel included or relaxed, especially when talking to strangers or officials. Good networkers are able to communicate effectively in a variety of modes, using a wide repertoire of communication styles ranging from formal report writing right through to the subtleties of cross-cultural body language. Conversation is an important way in which the community worker finds out about community concerns, hears about developments and is able to pass this information on to others. People's willingness to engage in conversation is affected by a number of factors, not least whether they like and trust the other person. Informal networking allows people to shift between roles while maintaining a clear identity and sound ideological base. The panelists were convinced that their ability to form relationships was about being 'straight-forward', neither having nor suspecting 'hidden agendas'. They felt that others saw them as honest, trustworthy, reliable and sincere. They found people confided in them readily and seemed to respect their advice. They described themselves as approachable, using words like 'popular', 'charming', 'sociable', 'extrovert' and 'comfortable'.

The community workers in the Panel Study were able to identify personal qualities that they felt enhanced their networking. These attributes can be clustered according to Table 4.

Personality traits seem to have a significant impact on networking ability. This includes a commitment to perceive and value the whole person, showing interest, empathy and attention. Remembering personal details about community members, and making genuine efforts to understand different points of view helps to build respect within a relationship. Good networkers make a positive contribution at a psychological as well as a practical level. Being optimistic and reliable helps to maintain morale, while following through on conversations and commitments is vital to sustaining relationships. A good networker is oriented towards other individuals, seeks affiliations but values autonomy, is non-deferential and tends to be less tolerant of formal organisational constraints. Effective networkers exhibit many of the attributes that predict transformational leadership: self-esteem, consideration for others and intuitive thinking. They provide leadership and show entrepreneurial flair, but without (apparently) the drive for personal ambition or profit. Networkers need to be able and willing to defy conventions, break bureaucratic rules, operate effectively

Table 4: Networking qualities

Affability	Warmth, compassion, empathy, humanity, gregariousness, responsiveness, attentiveness
Integrity	Self-aware, trustworthy, reliable, realistic, honest, open in dealings with others, respecting confidentiality
Audacity	Relishing change and innovation, prepared to challenge authority, take risks and break rules
Adaptability	Tolerant of differences, enjoying cultural diversity, flexible, non-judgemental, open to criticism
Tenacity	Patience, persistence, being comfortable with uncertainty and stress

in unfamiliar (social) territory and establish personal contacts rapidly and smoothly. In community development, informal networking necessarily takes place 'off-stage', making connections and giving encouragement in order to manoeuvre others into the limelight or into positions of influence. It is unusual to claim credit for such interventions and consequently, the value of this work has often been overlooked.

Establishing contact and forming relationships

Not everyone is capable of managing large social networks, and not everyone wants to. There are costs to offset against the benefits, and some people are more adept at maintaining this balance. Relationships are sustained through opportunity, common interests and social skills (Garrett, 1989). The range and nature of social networks are affected by a number of factors, including class, gender, life roles and ethnicity. Relationships progress through various stages, passing from initial acquaintance through to any number of potential endings (Levinger, 1980). People adopt different strategies to express and consolidate interpersonal attraction (Duck, 1991) and learn, usually from direct experience, the skills involved in managing social interaction (Wall, 1998). In extensive studies of relationship formation, Duck (1991, 1992) demonstrated the importance of communication in regulating the social processes of adaptation and exchange. The transition from acquaintance to friendship involves strategic use of self-disclosure, sharing information about oneself and testing out levels of affinity (Fehr, 1996). The significance of 'everyday chit-chat' lies in the processes of mutual discovery and bonding through which credibility is established, attitudes are explored and uncertainties about the 'other' are reduced until those involved feel that they know each other and have a certain sense of mutual obligation. Many theories of relationships are based on examining how these move through different phases while remaining balanced for reciprocity (Gouldner, 1960; Ikkink and van Tilburg, 1998). Different abilities are needed to manage relationships during these different phases. People need to recognise and take advantage of opportunities to form relationships. They need strategies for encouraging likeable or useful people into their personal ambit, based on an understanding of how relationships might evolve. They also need social skills to maintain and repair relationships during periods of conflict or adversity. Good networking requires self-awareness, strategies for self-presentation and skills in establishing rapport in a range of situations.

While networking techniques are usually conscious (identifying useful connections, responding to gaps in the web, and so on), the actual processes of building relationships should be authentic, otherwise the links are perceived as ingratiating and worthless. The community worker might be a catalyst in the interaction, in the sense of making things happen while remaining relatively unchanged, but they have to be genuinely involved and to take responsibility for their own actions. Non-verbal cues are crucial, especially in the initial stages. Thus the telephone is preferable to letter writing, probably because more can be discerned about someone from their tone of voice. Face-to-face interaction allows communication of emotional signals through body language, such as smiles, shrugs and posture. Good networkers will pay close attention to the paralinguistic dynamics of meetings and group interactions.

"Why is it I can go into some situations and the vibes tell me to be cautious? Nobody's really said anything, nobody's done anything to make me think that, but there's just a look, an action ... and you just think be steady in this situation." (LM)

Although they are more time-consuming, face-to-face interactions featured strongly in panelists' descriptions of networking. These seemed to accelerate and enhance the development of personal relationships and commitments. Direct encounters often demand one's full attention and this usually makes the connection more memorable.

"I'm very aware of that and I think that all those things happen at the first meeting. It's almost inevitable that we'll have made a relationship and sometimes that's far more important than the actual business." (KT)

Non-verbal communication was regarded as important in consolidating relationships and interpreting someone's response.

"You're talking about whether or not people have eye contact through conversations, simple things like that or whether or not you're making judgements on the basis of personal behaviour, whether a person smiles, whether a person looks confused, whether a person looks happy, or whatever, there are a whole range of judgements there, about our personal effectiveness." (CT)

In the course of routine work arrangements, panels recounted how they would go out of their way to make occasional face-to-face contact, even where this was not necessarily the most convenient or 'efficient' mode of communication. Several expressed a preference for this form of communication and sometimes made an effort to visit someone in person, rather than communicate by 'phone or by post.

"Last week I decided to consciously hand deliver to somebody a piece of paper that I could easily have put in the internal mail ... I could have put it in an envelope, and I thought, no I'll walk across to that particular office with it because I'll be able to say 'hello' to whoever's in that office and just pick up on the gossip and news. That's quite a pleasant thing to do, but it also just nurtures in their minds the existence of the work that I do." (MW)

Others made a habit of 'popping into' or 'hanging around' places where there was a high probability of meeting people with whom they needed to maintain a link. One panelist described how she would occasionally drive home through a particular area in the hope of "catching a wave" with residents there, and possibly even stopping for a chat. Others described how they deliberately structured their work so as to be 'out and about':

> "I'm not office based, I don't sit behind a desk every day, I make 'phone calls, I'm proactive, I go out of my way to go and see people regularly, whether it's sitting having a cup of tea in someone's home, whether it's being invited to do that, whether it's making a prior appointment to go and do that, or it's because somebody has made a particular point of contact and I've responded by saying 'Yes, I'll meet you'." (CT)

Panelists described how they made themselves 'ubiquitous', 'accessible', 'welcoming' and 'friendly' and were extremely flexible in how they did this. Living locally was an advantage, but other strategies mentioned were 'having lunch in different places', walking between appointments where possible and generally using the same amenities (shops, pubs, transport and so on) as the people you wanted to network with. This approach creates possibilities of meeting people in ways that were neither intrusive nor overly formal. It is about being in the right place at approximately the right time, and then making good use of whatever encounters happen to occur. This is clearly strategic in that it involves knowledge about local customs and habits, good planning, but also responding to opportunities as they arise.

Box 2: Neighbourhood networking by bike

"As a neighbourhood community worker I made a point of delivering letters to local community members by hand, usually cycling around the area to do this and often stopping off for a chat if I happened to bump into someone who I knew was involved in some group or activities. When there were events or jobs to publicise, I went round the shops, the health centre, schools and offices of voluntary organisations and local statutory agencies to put up posters and leave copies of our newsletter. Invariably these trips would lead to conversations with people I hadn't encountered before, creating new connections and occasionally recruiting new activists and volunteers for our community organisation. Although this 'outreach' strategy was considerably more labour intensive than simply posting the letters or leaflets, I felt it was worth the time and effort because it got me out of the Community Centre and ensured that my networks were constantly refreshed and extended to include people who might not otherwise have come to the building. Cycling, rather than driving or walking, offered a good compromise between getting around and being able to stop easily." (author)

Making contact sometimes involves being quite audacious, for example 'buttonholing' a comparative stranger from the crowd of potential contacts and then rendering the connection memorable and pleasant, so that the other person also has an incentive to continue with it. This requires political 'nous' in being able to 'read' interpersonal dynamics and understand the power dynamics affecting an organisation or an individual (Baddley and James, 1987). Studies of effective management and leadership identify important personal qualities, such as vigilance in processing information about the social environment (Bryman, 1992) and sensitivity to the feelings of others (Bennis and Nanus, 1985).

Face-to-face encounters allow a more accurate understanding of what people really feel and think. Community workers need to be sensitive to these aspects of collective behaviour because they often have to make decisions about their own interventions. Networking requires both analytical and intuitive thinking (Hammond, 1980). This includes an awareness of how people are relating to each other and identifying potential areas of friction or compatibility. This sensitivity is sometimes referred to as intuition and seems to be an important quality for community development. In an early exploration of the community work role, Williams (1973, p 3) advocates the use of an "imaginative sixth sense" when "playing the networks". Many of the panelists felt that their ability to form appropriate links and relationships was based on 'hunches' about what was going on in social interactions. It has been suggested that intuitive judgements are one of the characteristics of expert performance, which use learning from previous similar experiences and unfortunately are largely inaccessible to technical analysis (Dreyfus and Dreyfus, 1986). At the heart of professional practice lies an "ineffable knack" that defies measurement and description (Heron, 1996, p 112). The ability to perceive and activate potential connections is one of the 'knacks' of networking. 'Haphazard hunches' emerge which cannot be entirely justified through a rational examination of the evidence but nevertheless seem to work in practice (Eraut, 1994). Just as experienced chess players perceive the position of pieces on the board differently from novices (DeGroot, 1965), so expert networkers are able to make rapid and sophisticated appraisals of complex and dynamic processes from their observations of informal interactions. These abilities and insights are not developed overnight, but through experience and reflection.

Maintaining and using connections

A crucial but sometimes neglected aspect of networking is the need to maintain reciprocity in relationships. This does not necessarily mean that within each and every transaction there has to be an equal balance of give and take, as this is not always possible. Rather it is more about maintaining an overall perception within the network that nobody is in charge and that nobody is freeloading. Relationships tend to be sustained if they are based on fair and equivalent levels of exchange. For individuals, the cost of maintaining the connections has to be more or less balanced by the benefits and there should be a rough reciprocity among those involved. Research suggests that relationships that lack this balance eventually dissolve or are deliberately terminated.

Although not every contact might prove immediately or obviously useful, nevertheless information about it should be retained. When a link can be established and appears fruitful, it needs to be nurtured. Panelists were adamant that this should not be left to chance. Business cards and leaflets would be exchanged and definite arrangements were often made to meet again. Alternatively, a way would be devised to consolidate the encounter with some form of contact. This might appear fortuitous, such as noticing and sending a magazine article that would be of interest to the other party.

> "My follow up is to ask them questions and to listen to find out what their interests are, what are their needs, to note them internally and sometimes on paper. I then find that I can follow those up. Whatever people tell you, there's some kind of reverse sod's law. If they are interested in matchboxes there'll be an article on matchboxes in your tray, newspaper, in no time at all and so I'm able to follow that up with something concrete." (KT)

Others talked about finding ways of demonstrating a genuine commitment to the other person's well-being or work. Equally they might arrange to be somewhere where they were likely to 'bump into' that person.

> "And if it's something about grassroots level within the community, then.... I would go out of my way to be in a place where that person was if I wanted to continue those links. I mean it may be just something simple like a coffee morning I know they always attend, or [that] they always go round to the shops at a certain time. If I needed to see that person and I wanted to build up the links with them to be the secretary of a particular group or something like that, I would go round it that way, sort of plan my actions but it appears casual." (LM)

Building trust, taking risks

Relationships do not just happen and often involve considerable risk. Learning to trust the other person involves being prepared to rely on their judgement and actions. An expectation develops that their behaviour and motivations will be more or less consistent. Shared interests and values provide a reliable basis for reciprocal and strategic exchanges. Gifts and favours express mutual attraction and/or obligation, and provide the vital interchange of enduring voluntary relationships (Fischer, 1982; Werbner, 1990). A balance between the parties involved is usually maintained informally, and not necessarily through material transactions. Conviviality (pleasure, humour, fun) and empathy are valued in themselves, and form the basis for a generalised social relationship whose key components are "trust, reciprocity, altruism, commitment, sacrifice, tolerance, understanding, concern, solidarity and inter-dependence" (Twine, 1994, p 32). Even apparently superficial courtesy represents an acknowledgement that our lives are connected – that our actions have an impact and that the feelings and behaviour of other people are likely to be influenced by what we do or say. This is especially important in situations where there are no other means of reciprocity or sanctions, for example transactions between passing strangers (such as in traffic or public places), or favours between people who do not have an equal capacity to give (for example, adults doing things for children). Saying 'thank you' recognises that the other person has *chosen* to assist, freely and without expectation of reward. It reinforces altruistic behaviour and maintains goodwill and civility without which we would have no sense of society or community.

Relationships are risky in that they involve both hazard (being let down or betrayed) and uncertainty. Relations of trust are important in mediating risk and are a necessary precondition to the exercise of collective power. Trust is developed over time and is renewed rather than eroded through use. It is cultivated in civil society through active, reliable and mutually beneficial cooperation (Benington, 1998). Between individuals this creates the basis for friendship and neighbourliness. At community level it translates into shared conventions or social norms that regulate interaction and coordinate activities. These micro-social contracts are created and maintained mainly through face-to-face interactions. They allow us to make decisions about whether or not to engage in collective action when it is possible neither to control the outcome, nor even to predict what it might be. Trust was a theme that emerged strongly in both research studies. The Bristol Festival Against Racism was made possible because the key protagonists had built up good reputations within the relevant networks and could be trusted to deliver what they were promising. Stakeholders were willing to contribute to the initiative because they believed their money, energy and effort would be used to good effect. They were prepared to commit organisational resources and their own credibility to what at the time was a fairly risky venture, both politically and in terms of its sustainability. For the panelists, trust had a number of interlocking components. It involved fulfilling commitments and being frank about one's own role and motives.

> "I think the openness is important because the process of networking is carried by people building up trust and relationships between each other. People can suss you out if you say something you don't believe, they know that, and if you say something that you do believe they know that as well. Because they see you in a lot of different circumstances and they see you in different kinds of meetings, they bump into you in the street, they see you at informal meetings, they'll see you making a report to a council committee, and the same message the same agenda might be expressed in different tones of voice in the different settings. But it can ring true whether or not you're saying the same thing in those different ways and the different settings to

people. It gets back to people.... I think you build up trust with people if you're straight with them about what's possible, what you think, what you disagree with, not promising things that you can't deliver." (MW)

Benefits and limitations

Once established, networks allow people to cut across organisational boundaries and gain access to facilities, expertise and advice. This enables problems to be solved quickly and without going through official procedures. Informal and reliable contacts save time and effort because they can be used to request or negotiate resources, especially funding, more easily, and to link individuals into relevant groups. Personal contacts also provide access to external professional guidance for specific pieces of work, for example in relation to legislation and grant applications. Reciprocal working relationships develop through regular participation in relevant events and activities; using contacts to build up interdependence by "giving as much as I receive", as one person put it. This includes offering knowledge and advice, as well as simply sharing information and skills. There were many forms and levels of cooperation referred to in the interviews. People are able to avoid formal procedures by calling in favours:

> "... trading in kind rather than having to account for them [which gives] flexibility ... anything that doesn't have to go through the accountants." (GrS)

This seems to be especially necessary for workers in the voluntary sector, and may represent a covert redistribution of resources between statutory or intermediary agencies and smaller community groups. Panelists emphasised that it was the personal aspects of relationships that eased the processes of multi-agency working. It allowed people to move through and beyond the formal bureaucratic procedures to establish genuine mutuality, rather than 'paper' partnerships. People used their networks to cross organisational boundaries to solve short-term problems and to develop a collective response to common issues. Cooperation need not always entail direct collaboration. It may simply be about making sure that activities augment or complement each other. Networking with other organisations is useful for ascertaining the current 'state of play' and adjusting one's activities accordingly, for example to avoid competition for funding.

> "We contacted other people doing a similar sort of bid; not to pinch what they were doing, but to find out what their experience was and what their particular need was. We wanted to ensure that we weren't all making the same competitive bid which could penalise all of us." (JM)

Helpful connections can be nurtured, avoiding unnecessary (and wasteful) rivalries. Multi-agency partnerships and intermediary bodies are important in providing opportunities for this kind of coordination. As we saw in Chapter One, networking is a natural and ancient process that has made humans successful cooperators. Like any aspect of behaviour, it gets better through practice and can be used for personal or collective benefit. Within the context of community development, networking underpins all forms of community activity and should be seen within the framework of values set out in Chapter Two. However, networking can also be a self-promoting, manipulative and superficial way of getting ahead in life through the use (and abuse) of contacts by 'schmoozing' and 'name-dropping' for personal gain. Community development workers need to be alert to these tendencies and adopt strategies to counter them. Networks in themselves do not guarantee improved decision making or better access to information. Their informal nature and lack of mechanisms for resolving conflict or ensuring a balanced representation means that their membership is frequently unaccountable and exclusive. If left to their own devices, recruitment and communication within networks is biased towards those 'in the know' or whose 'face fits', while those who might bring a different perspective may be surreptitiously, but systematically excluded (Mayo, 1997b). Networking usually relies on informal processes and personal perceptions. These are based on local conventions, which in turn reflect the convenience and comfort of those already involved. Networks can reinforce prejudices and elitist practices when they operate predominantly on the basis of cliques, rumour and coincidence. A proactive and strategic approach is needed for community workers to counter these tendencies, using what Newman and Geddes (2001) call 'positive networking' to ensure social inclusion within partnerships. It is here that community development, with its core values of equality, solidarity and participation can play a role in creating and maintaining accessible and diverse networks.

Relationships as women's work?

Networking demands a complex range of capabilities, including social skills to maintain and repair relationships during periods of conflict or adversity. In addition it needs an appreciation of the social context and a willingness to intervene actively in order to assist other people to make their own relationships. In many informal networks there often seems to be one individual who keeps in touch with the others, who arranges get-togethers, has up-to-date news and contact details and generally ensures that everyone stays on more or less good terms. In families this role is often played by women, and there is evidence that women's emotional labour creates and maintains networks within other social settings, such as the workplace or within communities (Wellman, 1985). In the community work literature, networking is sometimes referred to as a 'womanly' way of operating (for example, Dominelli, 1995; Bryant, 1997). Studies have frequently commented on the role played by women in neighbouring and informal networks (Young and Willmott, 1957; Chanan and Vos, 1990; Bourke, 1994), running voluntary and community activities (McCulloch, 1997; Doucet, 2000; Krishnamurthy et al, 2001), participating in regeneration partnerships (May, 1997), sustaining solidarity and self-help, building inclusive political coalitions (McWilliams, 1995; Fearon, 1999) and generally keeping the peace (Kolb, 1992). More controversially, Stackman and Pinder argue in their study (1999) that gender differences appear in men's and women's work-based networks with the latter being more 'expressive' and based on relatively intense emotional ties, while men tend to cultivate fewer, but more instrumental links with colleagues. Other studies suggest similar patterns in conversation and community connections (Tannen, 1992). This chimes with Ferree's (1992) view that women tend to derive their motivation and identify from the web of attachments in which they are embedded.

Equally controversially, it is sometimes argued that women managers have a different, more egalitarian style of leadership that emphasises active listening, building relationships and respecting different views. Helgesen (1990, p 56) refers to this as the "strategy of the web" with its emphasis on nuturing connections in order to deal with ambiguous information. Networking is a means of gathering intelligence from a wide range of sources and using connections to learn and to persuade others to one's point of view.

Whatever one's position on the importance of gender in the range of skills and experience that underpin networking, it is clear that these abilities can be, and should be, acquired through observation and experience. Everyone can become more skilled and strategic in their networking. It is not my view that women are necessarily or instinctively better networkers, rather that this work of building, maintaining and mending relationships should be valued more (cf Hochschild, 1993). As we shall see in Chapter Eight, networking abilities are acquired in complex ways: from role models, practice situations, and possibly, formal training courses. Simply being more aware of techniques, traits and tendencies that support effective networking will encouraging people to adopt this approach more explicitly in their community development work.

Conclusions

This chapter has indicated the key elements and tactics for successful and sustainable networking. It has emphasised the importance of interpersonal relationships and face-to-face interaction, arguing that the work involved in networking should be properly appreciated as contributing to the development of community capacity and effective partnerships. The next chapter examines the specific contribution that community development workers can make to these processes through assisting people to make connections that might otherwise prove difficult or fragile.

SIX

Networking for community development

You have to go by instinct and you have to be brave. (from Anderson, 1995,
How to make an American quilt)

Introduction

Interpersonal relationships within the community and between organisations
need to be given greater significance to ensure that they are developed and
maintained in ways that contribute to the overall work programme of individual
workers or agencies. Networking clearly involves both 'common' courtesy
and good communication. It is about maintaining a web of relationships that
can support a useful and empowering flow of information and influence. Having
looked at the skills and strategies of networking, this chapter will examine how
these are used for community development practice. In particular, it will show
how community workers facilitate the networking of others, whether colleagues
or members of the communities they work with. It looks at what community
workers actually do to establish and maintain connections that are useful to
themselves and others. What aptitudes are required and what strategies are
deployed in a networking approach to community development and how might
these be acquired? What tangible outcomes are there to suggest that networking
benefits community members and makes community workers more effective?
There will be particular emphasis on the creation and use of links that span
organisational and community boundaries in order to promote partnership
working and community cohesion. The idea of meta-networking is introduced,
looking at the role of community workers in 'networking the networks' and in
devising opportunities for people to meet and work together.

Community development often feels somewhat nebulous, creating capacity
and cohesion from unpromising beginnings. Good networking practice requires
planning and proficiency; and can therefore fairly be described as work. It
supports collective action and sustains mutual cooperation, especially during
periods of conflict and demoralisation. Many of the difficulties and frustrations
faced by community workers derive from their position on the edges of
organisations. They are "everywhere and nowhere" (Miller and Bryant, 1990,
p 323): marginalised, misunderstood and yet in constant demand as mediators
between different agencies or groups. They 'network the networks', forming
boundary-spanning links across which information and resources flow to where

they can best be used. This role is rarely acknowledged, yet it is crucial to community development practice. Good community workers act not as gate-keepers, but as signposts and bridges, helping people through the barriers and navigating 'safe' routes over unfamiliar or difficult terrain.

Networking as practice

The use of 'network' as a verb is a relatively recent, but rapidly popularised term, which quickly produced its own parody in the question: 'Is it networking, or not working?'. There are very few formal definitions available, although Hosking and Morley's statement that "networking is a social process in which actors move around their decision making environment to build their own understanding and to mobilise influence" captures significant features of the practice (1991, p 226). There has been a sea-change in the use of the term and networking has been increasingly recognised as a vital aspect of community development work (cf Gilchrist, 1995; Taylor et al, 2000; Wilson and Wilde, 2001; Henderson and Thomas, 2002).

In recent years, job adverts and person specifications have frequently included 'networking skills' as a requirement, and posts have been created specifically to develop, coordinate and manage networks, indicating the value attached to this way of working, especially within the voluntary sector. Networking has even been identified as a measure of quality standards in the management of voluntary organisations (Gann, 1996), and Payne (1993) argues for linkages with social care programmes, referring to the need for regular liaison meetings and participation in local and national networks in order to share information and develop joint services. There are few other acknowledgements of networking as an indicator of 'good practice' from a management point of view, but see Gilchrist (2003a).

Nevertheless, among community practitioners there is a rising enthusiasm and interest. Interviews with the community workers in the study revealed the amazing vitality and richness of networking, with comments such as "absolutely central", "the start of everything", "the life and breath", the "sap" of community development, and "pretty vital to all of it". Networking was seen as a core process of community development, and also a key purpose.

> "Community development happens through networking.... I think the process of community development work is a process of developing relationships with people and encouraging people to build relationships with each other which are for the purpose of getting things done, but which will also have the benefit of educating people about the way in which they can best live together and to how they can best relate to sources of resources and power.... So the way you do community development work is through this kind of multidirectional process of relationship building which is networking.... It's essential. You couldn't do it without networking." (MW)

The community workers in this study deliberately allocated time and effort to develop and maintain their networks.

> "I consciously in my own mental work plan, say that I must spend a certain proportion of my time networking and proactively setting up networks of different sorts." (GrS)

They were often tactical about who they formed links with, careful in their approaches to different people and conscientious in monitoring and maintaining connections. People acted with design.

> "I'm strategic ... in the sense of almost making a list and saying 'Who do I need to pay attention to next?'. 'What network do I need to invest some of my time and energy into next?'." (MW)

Community workers in the Panel Study took risks and were extremely proactive in making contact with others. But they were also pragmatic and opportunist in their use of happenstance encounters and conversations. Networking was both serendipitous and strategic in the sense that the workers deliberately created or sought out occasions where they were likely to make useful connections. Panel members were skilful in their networking and flexible in applying different techniques in different situations. Responses to my interview questions often began with the phrase, "it depends..." followed by a sophisticated appraisal of the context and purpose of interactions, including explanations of why one approach would be more appropriate and effective than another. Nevertheless, there was considerable agreement that effective networking involved certain core organisational skills, loosely clustered around communication, interpersonal relations and knowledge management. After all, as Milson (1974) observed, "good organisation ... is a way in which we care for people. Efficiency is not the opposite of affection, but one of its expressions".

Promoting participation

Community and inter-agency networks can and should be vehicles for empowerment, affording greater access to decision makers and facilitating the emergence of community leadership. Community development aims to empower disadvantaged people through collective self-organisation. Identifying allies and building coalitions around a common vision involves working across a range of different experiences and perspectives to find (or create) a working consensus. This requires imagination and diplomacy. It is rarely a straightforward matter of aggregating the separate parts.

> "It's really difficult but ... often those people with completely opposite values can actually develop a relationship because there might be some other common issue that they share and eventually the fact that they're a different

colour or different sexuality doesn't matter.... They may have an interest in a piece of land that they didn't want to see destroyed and they work together on that." (TD)

Assisting people to 'self-organise' on the basis of a shared interest or oppression can be regarded as a legitimate form of consciousness-raising and empowerment. Networking is used to identify and to recruit individuals likely to be useful to collective ventures. 'Rising stars' are nurtured, community members cajoled into new activities and potential volunteers or management committee members solicited. This is particularly necessary in the early phases of developing a project or setting up a new organisation.

> "We set up discussion meetings to which we invited people who we thought would be interested in the idea. Before and after those meetings we chatted people up [...] and sold the idea to them, sometimes through letters, sometimes meeting people over coffee." (MW)

At community level, informal conversations support a constant process of matching interests, needs and enthusiasms. One-to-one work with individuals might be followed up with suggestions that they join a particular group.

> "If I think it would be really good for them to be involved in that, I'd say to them, 'Oh you should know about this, this is the person to contact to invite you to the next meeting', and then I ring the person who I suggested they contact and say 'Oh I met so and so the other day and I've suggested they phone you, I think they would be really good to invite along to this next meeting'." (FB)

The 'grapevine' offers an efficient and far-reaching means of gathering participants for community activities. Social networks appear to be more effective than posters, leaflets and newsletters in mobilising people for collective action because of personal motivation and a sense of shared risk. However, it is important to use public forms of communication as well to ensure that information is available to everyone you might want to attract.

Networking can be used to lobby decision makers around specific concerns and as a means of building people's capacity to influence decisions that affect them. Panelists admitted to using personal connections with policy makers to promote particular points of view, but they also saw their role as enabling other people to develop their own links with powerful bodies.

> "It's processes which empower people to be more able to voice their own views, to shape their own lives, their own organisations. That's the driving principle. So when you're networking ... the particular outcomes that I'm aiming for are things that I think will strengthen the ability of the local

community to represent itself and to get resources for itself and to develop a relationship with big power agencies like the local state." (MW)

Community networks are a means of developing a collective, but not necessarily unanimous voice through which different views and interests can be channelled. A more formal kind of networking is to create community forums that can be used as part of public consultation processes, although constant work is needed to make sure that these remain genuinely representative, transparent and accessible.

Meta-networking

In community development, good networking is about developing and managing a diverse array of contacts and relationships. Workers make judgements about how best to initiate and support useful links between themselves and others, and more importantly, use these to help people make and maintain connections between each other. This latter function can be termed *meta-networking* to indicate that it is about the work involved in supporting and transforming *other people's* networks. It represents an essential contribution to the development of the 'well-connected community' (Gilchrist, 1999, 2000). The concept of 'meta-networking' will be explored further in the concluding chapter, but for now the key components of effective meta-networking can be identified as:

* mapping the social and organisational landscape;
* initiating and maintaining interpersonal connections through referrals and introductions;
* managing and monitoring relevant networks;
* anticipating and dealing with tensions within and between networks;
* encouraging and supporting participation in networks where there are obstacles or resistance; and
* assisting in the development of structures and procedures that will ensure that networks are inclusive and sustainable.

Meta-networking is especially important if the social environment seems alien and fragmented or if people lack the confidence or the skills to initiate contact for themselves (Amado, 1993). This might be due to cultural differences, impairments, prejudices, power imbalances or perceived conflicts of interest. Community workers can facilitate these processes by finding connections, challenging preconceptions, creating opportunities for shared activities and encouraging dialogue across apparent boundaries.

Box 3: Networking for women's health

A chance conversation between two community workers, one based in a community centre and the other in a health promotion project, led to a group being formed to organise an event for local women to take part in activities at the local health centre. Using personal and professional networks, individuals and organisations were contacted, offering various enthusiasms and expertise around women's health. As a result a range of activities were available on the day, reflecting different cultures and traditions, as well as input from mainstream services. These included information about healthy eating, a relaxation class and a chance to learn something about the sociology of women's health across the world. Widespread publicity ensured that participants were drawn from different spheres and the informal atmosphere allowed people to discuss ideas and share experiences across the usual boundaries between academics, health professionals and community members.

Because meta-networking is about assisting the networking of others, it requires a working knowledge of shifting power dynamics and allegiances. Given current social inequalities, meta-networking also includes the use of positive action measures to overcome practical obstacles or oppressive attitudes. The worker's own networks provide an 'intangible resource' that can be used to build 'bridges to participation' (Rees, 1991; Mondros and Wilson, 1994) and this means they must take care to ensure that these are as inclusive and diverse as possible.

One community worker felt that it would be difficult to initiate effective collaboration:

> "… if there isn't the infrastructure of networking, if you don't know who is around and could usefully be involved in partnerships. Again I suppose it's the information and knowledge in the first place, then the personal contact." (GrS)

One of the major benefits of knowing how networks operate and having a mental map of the relations and attitudes of individual members, is the ability to place information carefully in order to influence decisions and enhance the likelihood of particular outcomes. In developing multi-agency working, it helps to know who in an organisation is likely to respond favourably to an invitation so that sympathetic individuals can be targeted within a larger bureaucracy in the hope that they would either contribute themselves or find a suitable alternative from among their own contacts.

> "I've got to try and get all the people there who I think should be, so then I would be quite strategic, suggesting specific people who would be useful to invite from specific organisations…. Because if you just send a blank letter up to the agency, the chance of anybody picking it up is kind of minimal really." (FB)

Networking involves forethought, sensitivity and a thorough knowledge of the context, including knowing how to engage someone's attention. Community workers are often points of entry to other networks or more formal systems using a personal link to make it easier for people to access the specialist help they need.

> "I think referrals to be effective need more than information ... but there is no guarantee they'll follow it up. It's much better if you can say, 'well I'll 'phone my mate Fred and say that you're here and while I'm on the 'phone you can make an appointment to go and see him', or whatever, and in some cases with particular sorts of people it's actually better to go along with them." (GrS)

Importance of informality

In community development, as in life itself, the formal and the informal are inextricably and symbiotically enmeshed. Networks operate through informal interactions and this is key to their effectiveness. Formal events can be useful for networking, not primarily because of the items on the agenda, but in order to obtain contacts and advice. The discussions 'around the edge' of the meetings are often more productive than the main business and are a way of exploring how people stand on different issues. Equally, meetings are occasions for fostering links in the professional network and maintaining one's profile. Even in these formal situations, humour and informal remarks reveal paradoxes, ambiguities or potential resistance (Berger, 1997). Network gatherings are usually characterised by an informality that allows people to talk directly across organisational and status boundaries on a seemingly more equal basis. The absence of formal structures and procedures allows people to be candid in their comments. This was identified as a major advantage of one network's meetings.

> "People have also said that they have been able to say what they would not [otherwise] be able to say ... because they're not seen as representing their organisation really, so they can say things about their own department that they wouldn't say in a formal situation perhaps." (PH)

The development of more personal relationships provides the durability and flexibility of many community-based organisations.

> "I think it's at the informal level that you build up trust and real relationships and this is absolutely crucial to bringing people together.... It's not just people, ideas and resources ... the informal networking is absolutely crucial, not only because you need it in a practical sense but, I think, because it actually reflects community." (KT)

The Festival Against Racism illustrated how informality made it possible for people to become involved on their own terms. This is important for community development, which relies on the voluntary engagement of community members. Informality encouraged spontaneity and commitment while paradoxically creating a sense of security. People use their informal networks to check things out, and then are able to make a more informed decision. The situation feels less risky, reducing the sense of trepidation and is experienced as empowering. One organiser described it thus:

> "If the approach is informal, the person being approached can measure their involvement, whereas if it's some kind of formal invitation you either make a commitment or you don't, whereas if it's informal you can bargain around how much commitment there is. It doesn't feel difficult in an informal setting." (LC)

In organising the Festival Against Racism a lack of bureaucracy released people's initiative and imagination.

> "People were not being regimented into any kind of structure I suppose ... I think that therefore people were able to be a lot more creative.... They could feel free and I think people tend to be a lot more responsive that way.... [They] didn't feel pressured. They felt trusted to come up with the right thing." (RS)

Informal methods of organising require less explicit commitment and provide easy escape routes. Informal encounters allow people to explain, to elaborate, and to explore what might have happened at a formal level (Laguerre, 1994). Informal interactions are used to clarify ambiguous or contrary interpretations of events.

> "People stay behind and talk to you and check out: 'How do you think that went?', 'What went on?', 'Who said what?', 'How do you think...?'. I'm checking out, reviewing and evaluating what's going on, making sure I've been to the same meeting as everybody else. Checking out what's happening." (GaS)

Seemingly casual comments or encounters are often neither observed nor recorded, evading surveillance by the authorities. Consequently, these exchanges appear to be more sincere, revealing what others really think as opposed to the official 'line'. Subversive or downright bizarre views can be voiced, usually resulting in further contentious or creative discussion. Informal conversations are where news is exchanged about personnel changes, the results of funding applications, or a chance to 'float' projects that are still only sketches on the mental drawing board. Advance notice of proposed policy changes travel the 'grapevine', and can sometimes be 'reformed' even before they are formulated.

Networking as information processing

Networks operate as irregular and informal lattices of interconnected people that cascade ideas and information out to different organisations and communities. Community workers are important nodes or relays in this communication system because they are in touch with many different groups. This is especially valuable around complex areas of knowledge or contentious issues, where a range of perspectives bring additional knowledge and understanding. Panelists were conscientious in using networks to convey information to where it could be useful, thinking about:

> "how to use what knowledge I've got and pass it back, because I really do believe this thing about information is power and that's part of networking." (SM)

They noticed and passed on items of news, not always immediately but saving it for the right opportunity or target. Receiving and storing information is an important area of competence, notably asking questions and really listening to the answers so as to notice (and remember) potential connections.

> "Sometimes it's just storing that little bit of information away in my brain, and it might not be apparently of use to me at that time, but I am aware that sometime in the future it might be of use to me or someone else." (FB)

This aspect of networking practice ranges from simply transmitting information, through to convening and servicing network-type organisations. Community workers are a resource that others use to obtain information. One community worker referred to their role as a conduit through which information flowed, as well as acting as a databank for other groups and the media. They become a kind of human encyclopaedia of local knowledge, "a walk-in file index" as one person described herself, but one which functions actively as a key node in a vast communication system.

Box 4: Networking to share ideas and information

"As a community worker, I often found myself as the first point of reference for enquiries about activities and organisations in the local neighbourhood. This was partly because the community centre was an obvious place to get information. We received newsletters, leaflets and directories from a variety of other bodies and usually were able to sift and make available the information contained in these. However, I also acted as a contact for less tangible appeals for help and my opinions were sought around a variety of issues. These requests seemed to come from right across the city and when busy, I found it mildly irritating having to stop what I was doing for the neighbourhood in order to focus on wider questions. However, I came to realise that by responding helpfully I was investing in a network of relationships that would in turn prove useful to me when I needed advice or information that was not available within the immediate community. The conversations also provided an opportunity to learn more about what was happening in other areas of the city and to gain more of an overview of policy developments or funding opportunities. This knowledge would naturally and eventually benefit projects and people in the neighbourhood where I worked." (author)

Good administration is a neglected aspect of effective networking, using notebooks, filing systems, card index boxes, diaries and address books to keep records and contact details. Obviously there are limits to the amount of information one person can be responsible for, so talking to colleagues and membership of various umbrella organisations are vital for staying up to date with the latest issues and news. Making time to read the relevant minutes, newsletters and periodicals is also important, although being on dozens of mailing lists can result in information overload, particularly in these days of computer-mediated communication.

Widening horizons

Informal networks are a source of inspiration and challenge, supporting a constant exchange of information and opinions. They enable people to gain an overview of situations and debates, gather useful insights, establish the 'bigger picture' and identify disparities. Networking is a way of monitoring reputations and making an appraisal of the links between groups. This is helpful at an individual level and contributes to the construction of a communal model of the world that can be used to determine collective strategies for change. Networking enables community workers to intervene directly in political or social processes, and to advise others on how these can be influenced.

"You've kind of got a sense of where people fit on the map of networks and you have a sense of where you fit ... you gradually build it up and you hear different and contradictory things from different people and you form your own judgements. So it's a gradual process of becoming part of that landscape of relationships, networks and power dynamics." (MW)

For community members, networking extends horizons and broadens perspectives, enabling people to gain an overview of the (policy) context and develop a broader understanding of issues. Networking enables people to stay in touch with shifts in the organisational field, as well as the dynamics of community politics. It is especially useful for obtaining unofficial views to compare with the public pronouncements.

Exchange visits between similar organisations encourage the transfer of ideas and learning from one community to another, so that they do not need to 'start from scratch' in setting up a project. This means that groups are:

"... not inventing the wheel all the time. Somebody has done something, they can learn from that, they can learn from other people's mistakes so they don't make the same mistakes, they can go one step further." (PH)

Groups discover that local difficulties may be part of a broader problem that neighbouring communities are also facing.

"I try and keep in mind that we've got to learn from other people's experience, locally and wider. Keeping ideas coming; and of course that's key and crucial to networking anyway. It's one of the purposes of getting as broad a spectrum of experience together as possible so that you can compare, contrast and learn." (KT)

Negotiating differences

As well as identifying areas of common interest between groups and between individuals, networking ensures that community members have access to a diversity of views, skills and knowledge. This may involve some ingenuity and a certain amount of risk in bringing together experiences that could be mutually challenging. Building bridges across perceived community or organisational boundaries is a first step in generating a dialogue, which might eventually break down barriers of fear, prejudice and antagonism. Networking creates occasions and spaces where people can learn from one another to develop greater tolerance and understanding. Judicious assessments may be needed about when and how to bring people together in situations that match their level of comprehension and commitment, and when to withdraw so that people can manage their own interactions. A major aspect of community development practice involves supporting communication and cooperation across psychological edges and organisational boundaries. This may include direct introductions at pre-arranged meetings or visits. It might also involve accompanying people to events and assisting them to make contact with those who might be useful to them by:

"... trying to break the ice between people ... making connections between people and convince them that talking to a particular person is a good idea.... I'll encourage people to come to a meeting perhaps because I know that somebody else is going to be at that meeting that they could make use of so it's generally not just a 'spur of the moment' thing." (PH)

Networking inevitably reflects personal interests and prevailing dynamics so networks easily become exclusive and cliquey. Community development workers should use anti-oppressive practice to reduce practical barriers and political biases, and to support the contributions of people who are less confident or articulate. One panelist described how she would accompany people from the community on their first attendance at a formal gathering:

"That does happen more in the Asian community ... or young people maybe. They would ask to come along with me ... just to give them a bit of confidence really. I mean I don't when I'm there, hold hands with somebody all day. I mean I would deliberately not do that. I [would find an excuse] to move out the way, and give the people their own space." (LM)

Networking is not simply about cross-validation and corroboration. Panelists actively sought out views that would challenge their own interpretations by meeting with people in other organisations or from different backgrounds. If connections with like-minded people are important elements in the network, so also are those that bring difference and dissent. And it is precisely these links that require more effort, more diplomacy and more imagination. This is where the *work* of networking takes place: setting up and maintaining the links between different (and sometimes antagonistic) sections of society. Marginalised sections of the community may need additional or alternative strategies in order to connect them into existing networks, and this may mean challenging or circumventing dominant interests and cultures. One panelist explained, for example,

"... the homeless, the poor, the elderly, black ethnic minorities, women, children, elderly people, people with disabilities and mental health, new people to an area, for instance. So you're trying to take all of those on board. Sometimes it is noting in a network that I'm in that they're *not* there. Sometimes it is so that the network can get them in but sometimes it is just reminding ourselves that we need to also do something else. We need to go out and talk to these people as well, as well as the valuable work we've done in the network because it's not always possible to get them into a network." (KT)

Drawing in new perspectives seems to be particularly crucial in this respect. Community workers used connections outside the immediate arena of their work to inject fresh, sometimes challenging ideas. One community youth worker on the Panel justified her decision to become involved in other projects beyond the remit of her job thus:

"There is no doubt that [my experience] benefited the community of young people because they then got input that they would never have got if I'd stayed as a peripheral suburban youth worker, not networked into inner-city projects and current political thinking and stuff like that.... If networking brings something new then it has to be a good thing, even if it's a different perspective and ... that is a product of having bothered to go out of your usual circle." (SM)

Another panelist contrasted the outlooks of two clubs for older people, only one of which was prepared to make links beyond their immediate membership. Its members:

> "... are prepared to listen to others, to learn from others, to contribute themselves, so it's a two-way thing which makes this communication important.... This need to want to listen to others, to improve not just the thing you're involved in but your knowledge of things generally and a have a wider look. Is networking really just a wider look on things?" (LM)

As a result of their links with other bodies, such groups become more adaptable and improve their chances of survival in an unpredictable funding climate.

Managing diversity and conflict

Networking is used to mediate, translate and interpret between people and agencies that are not in direct or clear communication with one another. Community workers are frequently invited to act as intermediaries between opposing parties, using their role to find common ground. If their relationships are robust and authentic, then disagreements may be dealt with amicably and effectively. Conflict can be anticipated and averted or handled informally. Disputes often erupt in communal facilities where people want to use the same space for different purposes. Tensions run high and this seems to be particularly the case when young people are involved. One panelist described how she was able to contain the antisocial behaviour of local young people by relating to them personally. It was a:

> "... huge advantage because I know them [the teenagers] by their name ... especially if they're the kids that also can cause quite a lot of trouble.... The fact that they're not anonymous actually makes an enormous amount of difference, and also working with the detached youth workers makes a lot of difference.... [The kids] know that their behaviour is what we do not like, it is not them." (FB)

Informal discussions are often useful in addressing controversies without them becoming confrontational.

> "If there is another point of view which they have not taken account of.... You have to talk to people about that as well. So in that networking ... it's the place where differences of agendas, differences of opinion ... get had out." (MW)

In order to cooperate, organisations must acknowledge competing interests or divergent ideologies. There may be differentials in power and perceived ownership that the community workers have to be aware of and seek to minimise.

Diversity also creates the possibility of innovative combinations and adaptations.

> "Collective, collaborative action [is] a means to solve problems, to make changes. It's just being open to finding the new. This is what's exciting about having a mixed community. It sets problems when new people come in and there's a mix but one of the good things is that you might come up with new solutions because of that." (KT)

Getting people to work together who have different cultures, interests and social status is fraught with difficulties and tensions. Networks can be used to manage that plurality in very positive ways by building personal links and mediating between factions to overcome dogma and intransigence. It helps to demonstrate interest in other people and curiosity about different lives and cultures. Good networking values diversity and deliberately seeks out experiences that will educate and challenge. This 'breadth of spirit' is demonstrated through compassion, tolerance and patience. Networkers show respect, not condescension, and are willing to learn from others. Being seen as human, even slightly vulnerable, helps to build genuine links with others. So does generosity in sharing resources, time, skills and knowledge. People in the 'helping' professions need to remember that for networking to be effective and sustainable, it is as important to *receive* as well as to *give* in order to maintain reciprocity with colleagues and 'clients'.

Good meta-networking involves a capacity to communicate across a range of different cultures and perspectives.

> "The fact that I've got a multidisciplinary background helps me in a practical sense of being able to anticipate but I think more important is the theory that not everybody understands the same thing from the same set of words or concepts and having that in mind is really helpful when it comes to mediating. It leaves me open. I don't make a judgement." (KT)

Although diversity brings complications and challenges, it provides dynamic opportunities for comparison and debate. It promotes greater levels of satisfaction for those involved and has benefits for collective problem solving. A major role for the community worker involves convening and servicing groups which bring together individuals across organisational and identity boundaries to develop 'critical alliances' (Ledwith and Asgill, 2000). Such coalitions recognise and respect differences but nonetheless are able to find sufficient temporary alignment to tackle a common grievance or achieve a shared goal. Community development uses networking to identify and explore underlying patterns of causation that can form the basis for collective action.

Where disputes exist or are anticipated, it is vital to create 'safe space' for discussing contentious issues (Norman, 1993) and for members to have the opportunity to get to know one another personally. The experience of cross-community working in Northern Ireland and other situations torn by sectarian or ethnic divisions demonstrate the value of trust and informal relationships in peace-building and conflict resolution (Harbor et al, 1996; Johnson, 1998; Kuzwe, 1998; Veale, 2000). Tensions are inevitable within and between communities, but they generate an important impetus for learning and transformation.

> "I really genuinely believe that conflict is a really healthy thing ... for two reasons. I abide by that statement that says 'from conflict breeds consciousness' but also because in my experience if you constantly live your life with people of the same values and shared vision then you never tighten up your arguments." (SM)

In community development it is often necessary to challenge existing practices and assumptions. Networkers can use their connections to 'grasp the nettle', asking awkward questions or giving constructive criticism. Personal networks are an effective, but occasionally risky way of circumventing bureaucratic procedures, and undermining the rigidity of corporate culture.

Networking the networks

As well as maintaining their own links and relationships, panelists described an additional role of 'networking the networks'.

> "I think my networks work ... they are actually very diverse. There is some overlap with them but there isn't a very core tight-knit group. I'm sort of very conscious I'm the hub of lots of networks." (GrS)

Community workers deliberately and strategically maintain their involvement in a range of networks, adjusting the level of their participation to ensure that the range of connections reflects current and potential work priorities.

> "Networking the networks has become very much my job, initially by default – it had to be done like that ... linking past, present and future, these things are always very important to me but implicit rather than explicit.... I think I'm always bringing a broad overview." (KT)

Community workers often play a vital role in setting up and coordinating 'umbrella' bodies that bring together people and projects operating across a variety of settings and issues. Several panelists were active in convening and chairing such forums. They performed a 'behind the scenes' function: servicing meetings, maintaining membership lists, sending out mailings and providing a point of contact. Multi-agency networks facilitate exchange and discussion across organisational or geographic boundaries. Forums and federations and, to some extent, local associations (such as neighbourhood or parish councils) aim to represent different sections of a community and to articulate a particular perspective possibly to another coordinating body, such as a cross-sectoral partnership. Informal networks create opportunities for people to link up with others who may have different interests and identities and yet share some kind of common values or purpose. Their ability to function effectively is determined by the quantity and quality of internal and external linkages.

Conclusions

Much of the literature on community, organisations and networking highlights the importance of one-to-one personal relationships, developed at the micro-level of interpersonal skills or at the macro-level of structure and purpose. Less has been written about the meso-level of collective activity: establishing and managing effective networks that can be used for a variety of purposes, including collective problem solving, resource mobilisation, organisation development and social change. Traditionally community development has emphasised the role of the professional in establishing groups and organisations with specific aims and activities. The idea of meta-networking as a core function shifts the focus of practice away from formal arrangements to encompass more informal processes. It is another way of looking at the well-rehearsed arguments about the balance between 'goal' and 'process' in community development. Meta-networking creates and maintains the linkages within complex and dynamic situations that enable new organisational arrangements to emerge and adapt to changing circumstances. These two ideas of emergence and complexity will become important themes in the final chapters setting out a model of community development as working towards the 'edge of chaos' and exploring implications for policy and practice.

SEVEN

Complexity and the well-connected community

One must have chaos inside oneself in order to give birth to a dancing star.
(Nietzsche, 1878)

Networking can be used to develop the 'well-connected community' but why are networks such an essential aspect of community life? We have seen that networks are especially effective modes of organisation in managing chaotic and complex situations. They are based on relationships, not simply connections. The personal, emotional dimensions are important. The evidence from practice suggests that networking is a holistic process, involving a strategic interweaving of knowledge, skills and values and that it is a vital aspect of community development, in addition to supporting multi-agency partnerships and alliances that span organisational boundaries. This chapter uses complexity theory to present a model of interactive networks creating the conditions for the evolution of new and adaptive forms of organisation that make up a dynamic voluntary and community sector. Chapter Eight then explores key issues and dilemmas associated with a networking approach to community development and highlights some implications for policy and practice. Chapter Nine draws the book to a conclusion by setting out a model of the 'well-connected community', and making recommendations for ensuring that networking practice is both effective and ethical.

Networks serve an important function in society and patterns of interaction and connection are strongly related to what is generally understood by the term 'community'. This has important implications for community development as an intervention for managing social complexity and strengthening the web of connections (Amin and Hauser, 1997). Recent pronouncements from the European Union and government policy units, refer explicitly to 'social capital' as underpinning various 'public goods' such as health, cohesion, inclusion and economic regeneration (PIU, 2002). The idea of 'community' continues to reflect core values associated with a socially just and sustainable civil society, namely respect, equality, mutuality, diversity and (more recently) cohesion. Why does the desire for 'community' persist and remain so prevalent across all societies? How does networking contributes to the development and survival of a well-functioning 'community', equipped with the capacity for organising collective responses to shared problems?

Chaos in the community

Networks operate well within turbulent environments, managing apparent 'chaos' in ways that enhance creativity and promote innovative forms of cooperation. As we saw in Chapter Three, organisational studies suggest that network forms of organisation are very effective at coping with high levels of uncertainty and ambiguity (Easton, 1996). It seems (at least in the developed world) that we live in a society more diverse and fragmented than ever before, in which role boundaries are blurred and personal identities have broken free from traditional social categories. Communities can be seen as complex environments characterised by interpersonal connections, fluid social networks and small-scale, self-help groups and voluntary organisations. Ideas from complexity theory may help us to understand some of the more puzzling features of our social and organisational world (see, for example, Wheatley, 1992; Jaworski, 1996; Byrne, 1998).

Many community workers would admit that many aspects of their work are unplanned or unpredictable. Happenstance encounters represent familiar but unexpected opportunities for sharing ideas and information that may lead to a change of direction or a completely new initiative.

> "Often it's the accidental meeting in the street where something completely new comes up that wouldn't have come up in a planned way.... It's just that chance." (KT)

It is normal for there to be an element of serendipity in community development so community workers need the flexibility and confidence to respond opportunistically to events occurring outside of their intentions or control. Developments often emerge or flow spontaneously from chance happenings.

> "There's a strength in being organised out of informal chaos, I suppose." (CT)

An experienced community worker will relish these kinds of situations, excited by the synergy while providing some continuity and stability for those around.

> "People see me as that person who's always there ... as someone who holds everything together throughout masses of chaos ... you are seen as a kind of rock ... that people keep hanging onto." (TD)

Over the years, community development has argued against targets and performance criteria, asserting that intervention strategies must be non-directive and nurture organic development rather than impose an external agenda. This is the difference between the top-down imposition of rigid action plans with predicted outputs versus a bottom-up approach that works *with* the grain of the community, helping them to define and achieve their own solutions using processes that simultaneously empower and educate. Networking prepares the ground for community-led projects to emerge that meet perceived needs and actual circumstances. The linkages between people and organisations are a vital part of a community's capacity to act collectively and engage with public decision-making bodies. A well-functioning community is vibrant with many different groups and activities that are connected through a myriad of organisational links and personal relationships. These enable new forms of cooperation to become established and old patterns of solidarity to become embedded in the traditions of that community. When this state of connectivity is reached, anything can happen, and frequently does, because a variety of experiences and interests are 'interjacent' within relatively safe environments (Thomas, 1976). Small occurrences trigger much bigger events in ways that can be neither predicted nor controlled.

> "I do find that you're building up [a web] in terms of your networking. It is about outreach, it is about exploration ... but I get to a point where there's suddenly a critical mass of outcomes. I think 'yes, this is making a difference'." (KT)

This unfurling of ideas and energy is a vital, but misunderstood feature of community development practice that is exciting, generative and mildly subversive. Gladwell (2000) refers to a 'tipping point', when trickles of apparently unrelated events become a torrent of coordinated activity. He highlights the role played by 'connectors', people who appear to 'know everyone', and act as key nodes in a vast and complex network. The networking approach to community development locates this function at the heart of practice, with the community worker facilitating many of the more difficult connections that make up the complex web of community and interorganisational life. In effect, the community worker is creating and facilitating a mainly informal system of people and organisations who interact to influence each other's behaviour. As a consequence, collective priorities, policies and practices emerge that reflect a range of personal actions and attitudes.

Key elements of complexity theory

With this in mind, it is worth looking at theories about complex systems because there are some interesting parallels with how communities operate, and how voluntary and community sector organisations evolve over time. Complexity arises as "result of a rich interaction of simple elements that only respond to the limited information each of them are presented with" (Cilliers, 1998, p 5). Complex systems are open: they are affected by changes in the wider environment and they also have an impact on what happens around them. The basic tenets of complexity theory were derived concurrently across different scientific fields: quantum physics, artificial intelligence, embryology, socio-biology and meteorology (Waldrop, 1992; Lewin, 1993). More advanced theory has developed through the study of non-linear systems in which apparently insignificant events have far-reaching consequences (Gleick, 1987). The most familiar example of this is known as the 'butterfly' effect, whereby the flap of a delicate wing is said to precipitate a hurricane on the other side of the world.

Complexity theory assumes that connections between elements are subject to relatively simple rules of interaction (known as Boolean logic) and that, in the absence of central control mechanisms, local clusters exhibit only limited awareness of the total system. Each unit responds to signals received from its neighbours, and eventually the entire system settles into a state of dynamic equilibrium, featuring familiar, but unique configurations known as 'strange attractors'. The system has evolved, apparently spontaneously and without external interventions, from an initially random set of interacting elements towards stable patterns of self-organisation (Jantsch, 1980). The *actual* configurations that emerge cannot be predicted in advance, but they invariably adopt forms that are characteristic of the system, its components and operating environment. A fundamental feature of complex systems is that of overarching properties that *emerge* as a result of localised interactions. Such a 'property' appears to function as some kind of integrating mechanism by which 'chaos' is averted. Thus the coordinated flight of a flock of geese is the result of simple rules of interaction governing the relative positions of a multitude of individual birds and enabling them to migrate safely across continents.

The history of a complex system is significant because what happens in the present is influenced by responses and adjustments to previous interactions. Complex systems have a capacity to process and store information from a variety of sources and are thus able to 'learn' from the past and to adapt to changing conditions. This seems to be an important feature of complex systems. The neuro-physiological structure of the human brain is a prime example of a highly evolved parallel information processing system consisting of interactive neural networks that respond to and synthesise particularly salient input and memories to 'produce' our perceptions and behaviour (Bechtel and Abrahamsen, 1991; McCrone, 1999). It has been suggested that consciousness is the emergent property of a complex system of neural activity that integrates our individual experiences within the highly plastic, self-organising, but functionally specialist, structures of the brain (Dennett, 1991; Rose, 1998). It is not too far-fetched to envisage 'community' as the collective equivalent, creating both 'social identity' and 'social capital' through its ability to generate, receive, compare and disseminate human knowledge and emotions.

Complexity theory encompasses chaos theory and is concerned with understanding how 'order' appears 'immanent' (enfolded) within apparent chaos. It is observed that a complex system will, over time, adjust its arrangement of connections until it achieves a state of dynamic but stable equilibrium. Complex systems comprise a multitude of units (nodes), interacting in ways that are mutually influential, yet relatively 'local'. A state of chaos is said to exist where a large number of elements influence each other's behaviour to produce dynamic and *unpredictable* patterns of activity. Contrary to popular belief, a system in chaos is not operating at random. Nevertheless, since the probability of events occurring is affected by immediately preceding and neighbouring interactions, it is possible only to forecast likely trends, not to specify the detail of future events (Eve, 1997). A system's complexity increases according to the number of elements in the system, and the levels of interconnectivity. It is useful to imagine complex systems as ranged along a spectrum of activity from 'stagnant' (where nothing significant happens and there are no noticeable changes) to 'chaotic' (where every alteration in the pattern produces upheavals across the system) (see Table 5). Computer models of cell automata have been used to simulate the behaviour of complex systems. Kauffman (1993, 1995) identifies three broad bands of operation for these systems: 'frozen', 'melting' and 'chaotic'. Complexity theory suggests that systems with low levels of connectivity and highly similar elements freeze into static configurations. Populations that have these levels of fragmentation or homogeneity (either by choice or circumstance) are unable to innovate or adapt to changes in or around them. At the other end of the continuum, systems in which the behaviour of elements is influenced by many highly diverse connections are too volatile and cannot achieve stability. The optimal state for a system operating in an uncertain, turbulent world is in the 'melting zone' on the '*edge of chaos*'. This latter term was coined by the mathematician Norman Packard to describe an intermediate zone of 'untidy creativity', between rigidity and chaos, where the system is best able to function, adjusting constantly to slight perturbations but without cataclysmic disruption. A complex system at the 'edge of chaos' maintains itself in a state of dynamic equilibrium through processes of self-organisation, known as autopoiesis

Table 5: Spectrum of complex systems

➤➤➤➤➤➤➤➤➤➤➤➤ **Increasing levels of connectivity** ➤➤➤➤➤➤➤➤➤➤➤➤

	Static	**'Edge of chaos'**	**Chaos**
Nature of interactions	Frozen, stagnant	Vibrant, creative, adaptive	Unpredictable, volatile
Level of connections	Sparse, few boundary-spanning links	Rich and diverse, plenty of 'weak ties'	Saturated, high density networks
Community characteristics	Isolated from wider society and external influences; fragmented or homogeneous	Cohesive, social structures and informal networks are inclusive	Volatile, mobile or transient population, few linkages between clusters and sectors
Typical examples	Closed, long-standing community such as a monastery; rigid structures and strong centralised control	Multi-ethnic neighbourhood with fairly stable population, mixed tenure housing; range of self-help community groups and umbrella organisations	Unpopular peripheral estate, housing dominated by single social landlord, transient population; absence of formal structures and community activities

(Maturana and Varela, 1987; Mingers, 1995). The emergence and experience of 'community' achieves this for human societies, through the integrating and communication functions of informal networks.

Communities at the 'edge of chaos'

In human terms, groups and organisations crystallise and evolve in an environment of complex and dynamic social interaction. Studies of local voluntary activity, social movements and the community sector identify a degree of order and coordination within community settings, demonstrated at organisational level through mutual affiliation and liaison, and between individuals through friendship networks and overlapping membership (Curtis and Zurcher, 1973; Chanan, 1992; Tarrow, 1994; Taylor, 1995b). These mechanisms maintain a social system at the 'edge of chaos'. Whatever the basis for the connections between individuals, it is evident that networks are crucial to the development and maintenance of collective action strategies (Klandermans, 1997). People's sense of 'community', their social identity, derives from the unpredictable dynamics of mutual influence and interaction. This reflects real experience and emotions, encompassing the negative aspects of human relationships, as well as rose-tinted notions of belonging, trust and loyalty. Community is the 'emergent property' of a complex social system operating at the 'edge of chaos', ensuring cooperation and cohesion without imposing formal or centralised control. In this respect, 'community' is not simply equivalent to a 'social system', but rather the outcome of interactions within networks. 'Community' represents both the context and the process through which collective problem-solving mechanisms emerge, in much the same way as life forms evolved from the 'primordial soup' of previous aeons (Kauffman, 1995). The sociologist, George Herbert Mead, recognised this phenomenon many years previously, observing that

> ... when things get together, there arises something that was not there before, and that character is something that cannot be stated in terms of the elements which go to make up the combination. (1938, p 641)

This prescient form of systems thinking recognises that different properties appear at successive levels of analysis and are the product of 'organised complexity' (Capra, 1996). Complex networks are the pattern of all living systems, in which evolution uses chance and necessity to assemble new entities and to sustain diverse and resilient eco-populations. Those combinations that best 'fit' the current environment are those that survive. The precise format and membership of these cliques, clusters and coalitions are influenced (but not determined) by factors in the environment, such as public interest, political expediency, funding regimes and the existence of similar organisations competing for the same resources (Milofsky, 1988b). A familiar range of collective entities can be discerned in the groups, forums, federations, clubs and societies that populate civil society, and the voluntary and community sector in particular. These reflect prevailing cultural expectations, local conventions and often perpetuate existing differentials of power and privilege. These are the 'strange attractors' of complex mature systems that have evolved at the 'edge of chaos'.

'Community' was first proposed as an antidote to 'chaos' in a paper published just half a century ago by the National Council of Social Service (White, 1950). In Greek mythology, the gods Chaos and Gaia were regarded as inseparable and complementary partners, acting in tandem to maintain the world as a self-sustaining system (cf Lovelock, 1979). Using this framework, it is possible to reconceptualise the purpose of community work as helping to achieve Gaia-like levels of connectivity. This includes enhancing people's capacity to network individually and through their collective organisations. Traditionally in community development the emphasis has been on establishing and managing specific forms of association as goals in their own right. The 'edge of chaos' model of community suggests that the purpose of such activities is primarily to create opportunities for interaction. Community workers use networking to support joint ventures that in turn strengthen personal networks and enable complex interorganisational coalitions to operate (Shuftan, 1999; Bradshaw, 2000).

Creating opportunities for networking

Networking is an active and on-going process that flourishes more readily in some circumstances than others. Traditional community work activities, such as festivals, local campaigns or support for self-help groups, do not seem to be directly concerned with building relationships. Nevertheless they provide vital opportunities for informal networking and should be organised in ways that do not unintentionally exclude some people or perpetuate inequalities. Networking must therefore be based on anti-discriminatory practices that address issues around access (Byrnoe and Oliver, 1991), cultural appropriateness (Hopton, 1997) and the assumptions and feelings that constitute internalised oppression. Networking can be conceived at one level as a method of opening up and shaping communal places in order to facilitate integration and cohabitation while promoting equality and diversity (Nash and Christie, 2003).

Changing the structures and cultures of an event or organisation can radically alter patterns of interaction. Community workers' professional commitment to empowerment makes it necessary to intervene in situations so that people are more able and more likely to interact with one another in ways which promote respect, trust and mutuality. Attempts to involve people from disadvantaged groups should be genuine and practical, not tokenistic, and may require prior work to build confidence by supporting smaller, self-organised groups until they feel able to participate equally in wider activities and partnerships. It is likely also to require tackling oppressive attitudes and behaviours among people who assume (often unconsciously) privileged territorial 'rights' based on previous custom and practice. This can generate resentment, even outright conflict and must be handled carefully (Gilchrist, 1992a, 1992b). Above all, networking should protect people's autonomy and accommodate their diversity (Ling Wong, 1998).

Meta-networking strategies commonly involve food and entertainment. These might be regular opportunities to meet and mingle in a convivial atmosphere, such as a community centre cafe. Preparing and sharing food together is an enactment of 'communion' which exemplifies the origin of the word 'community' but, as Nelson et al (2000, p 361) observe, it is also a "gendered burden" mainly undertaken by women. Cultural and sporting activities (even competitive ones) are another means of forging closer links, perhaps because of their semi-structured and yet informal nature. Team-building exercises often use these activities to create situations for improving trust and cooperation among disparate groups. It has been suggested that many communal games were developed in order to express and diffuse tensions within a safe arena where roles are clearly defined and power differentials limited (Milofsky, 1988c).

Box 5: Networking through team sports

For a while the predominantly female staff team at a community centre played netball together once a week on Sunday afternoons. This was enjoyable and provided a regular opportunity to break down status and ethnic differences. Getting to know each other out of work roles consolidated already good relationships and contributed to a general willingness to help each other deal with minor problems and irritations in the centre. This resulted in a good atmosphere in the building and better team working.

Spaces and places for networking

Community spaces, groups and activities provide integrating mechanisms that are neither bureaucratic, intimidating nor remote. Community development seeks to create communities "which are inclusive, open and creative, and in which difference is welcomed and valued" (Warburton, 1998, p 17). Ecologists emphasise the importance of 'biodiversity' in preserving a sustainable global environment (Wilson, 1992). As Capra recognises in his model of the 'web of life':

> ... in ecosystems, the complexity of the network is a consequences of its biodiversity, and thus a diverse ecological community is a resilient community. In human communities, ethnic and cultural diversity plays the same role. Diversity means different relationships, many different approaches to the same problem. A diverse community is a resilient community, capable of adapting to changing situations. However, diversity is a strategic advantage only if there is a truly vibrant community, sustained by a web of relationships. If the community is fragmented into isolated groups and individuals, diversity can easily become a source of prejudice and friction. (1996, p 295)

Socio-diversity guarantees a continually enriched society, with all its contradictory values and experiences. For diversity to flourish, communities need neutral communal spaces, which are neither private nor public, where the integrative processes of community and civil society can be continually renewed (Harrison et al, 1995; Warburton, 1998). Schuler (1996, p 53) describes these 'third places' as having a playful, convivial atmosphere, where conversation is the main activity. They are accessible and accommodating to different people, feel like a 'home away from home' where there are neither guests nor hosts, simply regular users who share the space and engage with one another as and when they choose (Oldenburg, 1991). The importance of public places for community interaction is increasingly recognised by urban planners (Landry, 1995; Barton, 2000). Communal spaces provide arenas for social interaction that are not governed by overly formal etiquette but where safety, open access, cultural diversity and civic responsibility can be assured (Cooper, 1998). Factors such as traffic flow through local streets can have a major impact on the level and quality of community interaction (Appleyard, 1981) and has often been the target of community campaigns. The creation of traffic-free 'home zones' should be a consideration in planning designs for sustainable neighbourhoods (Barton et al, 2002). Familiarity and mutual recognition influence how users of public space relate to one another, but so also are expectations that local interests and cultures will be acknowledged, perhaps even celebrated. Such spaces can be designed and shaped (using community art such as murals or sculptures) to encourage processes of interaction which promote diversity and equality, rather than simply reflecting the dominant presence.

How can local spaces become genuinely 'communal' places which people use for specific purposes but where they will also encounter *on an equal basis* people with different needs or lifestyles? To some extent, community workers have always been involved in creating and maintaining 'third places' where people can meet for a variety of purposes or simply to hang out with friends (Twelvetrees, 1976, p 122; Gatehouse, 1982; Marriott, 1997, p 9). Community workers can help people to share such facilities, dealing with the inevitable clashes while encouraging conversation, integration and understanding. As many people living in mixed neighbourhoods will testify, co-residence does not guarantee either interaction or mutual obligation (Wallman, 1986; Cantle, 2001; Madanipour, 2003). Community workers can play a role in facilitating communication and cooperation where it does not occur 'naturally', building bridges between different sections of the population while trying to create (and sometimes defend) spaces for marginalised groups to empower themselves and affirm their own identity (Breakwell, 1986; Gilchrist, 2003c).

Communal spaces are where people meet regularly, exchange pleasantries and eventually begin to form low-intensity, but potentially helpful relationships. This may explain the enduring dominance of the geographical dimension to definitions of community. It reflects the importance of 'place' as a site for unplanned, informal interaction (Massey, 1994) but the tendency to romanticise the village or neighbourhood as the pre-eminent (if not only) basis for 'community' should be avoided. Perhaps we need to reinvent a (post)modern equivalent of the Italian 'passagiata', a regular promenade of citizens that encourages face-to-face interchange in an environment that has open access and few rules of engagement. Seen from this perspective, community festivals, village fairs, open days, street parties and similar events are vital activities in the local calendar because they encourage people from different organisations and the community to work together, strengthening the trust and ties between them. Just as significantly, such events themselves provide opportunities for 'ordinary' residents to participate in something that does not require a deep commitment, but brings them into contact with neighbours and other members of the community in a friendly, semi-structured and non-threatening environment. Community development workers play a key role in helping community activists to organise (and publicise) these events, and crucially, in ensuring that they are accessible and inclusive for all residents and potential visitors. It is particularly important that people from different cultural backgrounds feel welcome, and that the access requirements of Disabled people are met. Considerable hidden work is needed to ensure that such 'open' events are genuinely comfortable and relevant to all sections of the community.

Developing the well-connected community

The overall function of such interventions (whether by paid professionals, volunteers, social entrepreneurs or active citizens) is the development of a complex social system operating at the 'edge of chaos'. I have termed this model the '*well-connected community*'. Ideally this is based on flexible, self-reliant networks that contain, or have links to, a '*sufficient diversity*' of skills, knowledge, interests and resources for the formation of any number of possible groups and collective initiatives. The task of the community worker is to enable people to establish these connections and maintain the web. As Zeldin notes in championing the role of intermediaries, "respect cannot be achieved by the same methods as power. It requires not chiefs, but mediators, arbitrators, encouragers and counsellors ... whose ambition is limited to helping individuals to appreciate each other and to work together even when they are not in complete agreement" (1994, p 144). What people then choose to do with these connections will be affected partly by individual motives, partly by local circumstances, and partly by the social and political environment. The acknowledgement of 'chance' and emotion within the process does not diminish the influence of policy makers nor the skilled input of community workers. Instead it highlights the difficulties of accurate forecasting and the need for flexibility around evaluation. Community development cannot be realised through business plans or the achievement of specific performance criteria. Rather it is about helping a given population (social system) move towards the 'edge of chaos' as a way of managing uncertainty and developing shared infrastructure. This involves the establishment of dynamic and diverse networks to create patterns of interaction that are neither utterly confusing, nor frozen rigid.

A system at the 'edge of chaos' is immensely capable of responding to changes in the external environment. It is certainly not isolated from the outside world. Links that cross system boundaries offer a further advantage in allowing for the import of new ideas and comparisons between different experiences. 'Weak ties' provide the communication channels within communities, spanning boundaries and bridging divisions. The 'strong ties' support exchange relationships allowing resources to be shared and close bonds to develop. The 'well-connected community' has strong internal relationships, but also benefits from useful links with people and organisations beyond its immediate borders.

The principles of empowerment and equality can easily be incorporated into a complexity-based model of community development. Discrimination, prejudice and social exclusion are not just 'morally wrong'. They can be seen as dysfunctional in that they disrupt the free flow of information across the system and restrict the development of potentially advantageous collaborative arrangements. Equality issues must be addressed in order to dismantle barriers to communication and to promote diversity within the networks. Anti-oppressive practice promotes the *integrity, diversity and authenticity* of the whole system. This involves tackling institutional discrimination as well as attitude change, embracing political, practical and psychological levels of transformation (Ledwith, 1997, Thompson, 1998).

Conclusions

Networking and 'meta-networking' are fundamental methods of community development, and underpin core policy themes of cohesion and inclusion. Professional practice assists individuals in making strategic and opportune connections that create and maintain collective forms of organisation. In systems such as human society, 'community' reflects both the objective experience and the imagined 'spirit' of complex interactions, from which emerge the familiar 'strange attractors' of self-help groups and citizens' organisations. A sense of community expresses that dimension of our lives that is about tolerating difference, promoting equality and acknowledging mutuality. The present model of the 'well-connected community' does not attempt to reinvent a nostalgic version of traditional villages or urban neighbourhoods. Instead, it proposes a complex, almost postmodern vision of an integrated and dynamic network of diverse connections. The purpose of community development is simply to support and shape formal and informal networking in order to facilitate the emergence of effective and empowering collective action. As society becomes increasingly complex, the maintenance of interlocking flexible networks around a variety of interests and identities will constitute our best strategy for building mature, resilient and sustainable communities.

EIGHT

Issues and implications

Chaos or Community? Where do we go from here? (Martin Luther King, 1968)

It is now generally accepted that networking is essential to the community development process and that without it other functions that are more formally recognised as the purpose of community work become difficult or impossible to carry out. The SCCD Strategic Framework states that:

> Networking is important because it provides access to information, support, resources and influence. It enables cooperation between practitioners, researchers and policy makers in different sectors through the development of trust and understanding.... Community workers facilitate networking by putting people in touch with one another, by creating opportunities for people to meet, and by providing safe spaces for interaction and learning. (2001, p 20)

Community workers frequently hold pivotal positions or play a key role in setting up and servicing network-type organisations, such as area- or issue-based multi-agency forums. They provide 'maintenance' and 'leadership' functions, sometimes chairing meetings, organising mailings, monitoring and generally encouraging participation. In short, they establish situations in which networking flourishes, and work hard to ensure that these are inclusive, productive and equitable by paying attention to issues around access, reciprocity, diversity and power. This emphasis on networking raises a number of questions concerning the position and function of the community worker, which have implications for policy and practice. Informal networking complements formal liaison mechanisms by creating the conditions that support effective coordination across boundaries. The *connections themselves* appear to be a foundation for collective and individual empowerment. Sound working relationships are vital for joint action and collaboration. They create a collective power-base that enables individuals and groups in communities to influence the decisions of more powerful bodies.

Managing roles and accountability

Networking has been portrayed as an activity in which people engage as 'themselves' and the importance of 'authentic' relationships has been constantly emphasised. But, like any other profession, community workers need to maintain their accountability and standards vis-à-vis colleagues, employers and community members. As we have seen, trust and informality are important aspects for networking, and good practice must also consider issues around power, role boundaries and evaluation. Sustainable networks have to be based on genuine commitment and mutual interests. Community development workers use 'themselves' but should not lose sight of their responsibilities as agents representing their employers or as accountable to different sections of the community. In his examination of personal networks, Heald (1983, p 213) suggests that the "art of networking is to do it naturally and with pleasure", but for the professional community worker personal preferences cannot wholly determine the nature or content of useful connections. Good community development requires the maintenance of real and reciprocal relationships. Networking is effective for community development because it is *personal*, involving more than superficial connections devoid of emotional content. Networking is *not* about exploiting contacts in a manipulative or selfish way, but about establishing levels of trust, goodwill and mutual respect that run deeper than a sporadic and cursory exchange of information or favours. Personal relationships make it easier to make requests and suggestions, especially when these are inconvenient, complicated or hazardous.

> "The personal touches are so important. If the personal stuff and the foundations are right, then I think the work will come out of it, because people will have such faith in you." (TD)

This is particularly important when working with disadvantaged and oppressed people, who may feel more vulnerable and more suspicious of professional interventions. It is vital not to let people down or to deceive them. Being 'oneself' is crucial, while also taking care to negotiate and maintain role boundaries – a delicate balancing act. Adequate supervision and training would improve this, helping workers to be more conscious of role boundaries and better able to assert, or at least, manage these. The growth of multi-agency and multi-layered partnerships has accentuated this issue, making it ever more important that community workers are able to work across organisational boundaries while maintaining both professional identity and accountability. Professional networking usually needs to stop short of friendship and personal intimacy. This applies to colleagues as well as community members so as to minimise difficulties around confidentiality or misplaced loyalty that could distort decision making.

> "I try to make sure that I don't take advantage of somebody, because it's easy to mislead people into thinking you're developing what could be a friendship with them, when really what in fact you're doing is developing a working relationship.... I find this especially so in the mental health field, or people who are unemployed or just vulnerable for whatever reason." (TD)

Constantly 'being oneself' means that it is difficult to change or lower one's standards without being seen as hypocritical. The chameleon-like nature of networking also creates strain, in that:

"... you can't be all things to all people all of the time." (PH)

Notions of 'good practice' include attention to role boundaries, operating as transparently as possible, maintaining accountability and ensuring that relationships are balanced and non-dependent.

"Networking needs to take place at all levels [so that it is] mutual, it's supportive, it's not exclusive [and] must involve all sections of the community with different levels of experience. It needs to occur purposefully and explicitly." (CT)

This can create an additional burden for community workers in that this work is hidden from public view and can be taken for granted by others. It is not always appreciated that someone's capacity to provide relevant information and contacts has probably involved a great deal of time and attention in acquiring (and storing) that knowledge in the first place. Practitioners need to work hard at cultivating the less opportune or more uncomfortable links in their networks. This involves making efforts to stay in touch, to send apologies and to show a continuing interest towards different projects and communities. Networking can be stressful and precarious, creating hidden or un-negotiated accountability webs that can be confusing and onerous. This aspect of networking is often overlooked, and is the most probable cause of burn-out so often encountered in this type of work (Maslach, 1982; Ife, 1995). 'Burn-out' is very common in community development and appears to be the consequence of a mismatch between expectations of what can be given and achieved by the worker. It is characterised by emotional exhaustion and a reduced sense of personal accomplishment, possibly because the demands on 'well-connected' community workers can come from anywhere in their extensive networks, and because networking seems so much to involve using one's own identity and beliefs to build and maintain relationships. This can amount to a kind of 'prostitution of the personality', trying to be endlessly helpful, kind and caring to any and every member of the community.

This issue of boundaries and 'burn-out' is particularly relevant to discussions about whether community development work is best undertaken by people who are themselves community members or by outsiders. In these situations it is more difficult to demarcate 'work' from 'life', and some people prefer not to do this anyway, for example those working from overtly faith or political perspectives. In most work contexts a deliberate shift to informality can be used to indicate when roles are being blurred, by changes in the style of communication, relaxing of dress codes, and using alternative settings or timings. Within most professions and bureaucracies, work conventions are recognised and generally adhered to, and so this switch from formal to informal is obvious. But community workers have no 'uniform', often work 'unsociable' hours, occupy no fixed 'workplace', may themselves be members of the community, and would normally converse in everyday language. Experienced community workers develop tactics to distinguish between their professional roles and personal lives. At an interpersonal level it is probably all right to blur role boundaries but not to obliterate them altogether. The informality of settings and encounters is a crucial aspect of networking that makes it different from formal liaison and inter-agency collaboration.

Occasionally it may be expedient to dissolve the boundaries between paid and unpaid time, between activist and professional roles, and it is common for people in community development to be 'wearing several hats' at once. This multiplicity of ties and roles can be useful in terms of gaining access to different networks and building credibility but it also creates confusion around mutual expectations, confidentiality and professional accountability, especially when your friends and colleagues may also have formal responsibilities as your employers and managers, as is often the case in the voluntary sector.

> "Networking the networks is very much part of my job but networks have aims, have policies and so if I'm in a network I take very much on board what their aims and objectives are, what their policies are and I try and work within those." (KT)

Paid community workers need to be clear about their role as members or representatives of organisations especially within interdisciplinary teams or multi-agency partnership bodies. Nevertheless, participation in a network allows one to enjoy a degree of autonomy to make suggestions and take stances that might not be possible within a more rigid organisational framework.

Networking provides informal mechanisms of accountability. It allows people to monitor their own performance and credibility and provides a means of informal reporting. Managers should help community workers to clarify their roles and to review on a regular basis the effectiveness of their networking by asking people to examine how their relationships with people in the community are developing and being maintained. Otherwise the almost infinite complexity of informal networking can be somewhat bewildering for the workers *and* those they work with (Gilchrist, 2003a).

Preference and affinity

Networking is easier and more enjoyable where there are common interests and mutual affinity. People tend to associate with people who are like themselves, and this dimension of networking militates against inclusion and equality of opportunity. Understandably people will seek company and stimulation where they feel appreciated or comfortable, and this also applies to 'off-duty' community workers. Personal preferences should not be underestimated as a source of inequality in networks and this can have an unacceptable impact on community participation and joint working. The effect of envy, resentment, fear and repulsion on personal and professional networks has yet to be studied, but obviously these negative emotions affect the availability of ideas and resources within the community and voluntary sectors. Personal affiliations and antagonisms are endemic in community networks and this creates a quandary for people who are committed to principles of equal opportunity and democracy.

The term networking has been used disparagingly to refer to tokenistic interactions that are short-term, superficial, expedient and often elitist. In some quarters, networking has become 'fashionable', sometimes carried out solely to meet the requirements of current funding and partnership regimes. 'Bad' networking could take many forms. It might involve poor communication between individuals or a failure to understand how information will spread through a network. Networking could be both ineffective and unethical if it did not involve a balanced gain for all participants, and if it was not based on a level of genuine commitment. This is a superficial and unsustainable form of community development. 'Bad' networking would pay insufficient attention to gaps and inequalities, preferring to maintain only connections that are comfortable or convenient. Priorities and positive action to ensure equal opportunity within networks must be considered in order to minimise unwitting or deliberate biases. While it is feasible to keep information on a huge range of contacts, it is not possible to keep alive an unlimited number of links or relationships since these usually wither away unless actively maintained and must be constantly reviewed to take account of changing priorities and circumstances. Strategic judgements must be made about how to prune or nurture different bits of the network to avoid missing opportunities by over-attentiveness to the 'wrong' people. Opportunities for unplanned networking need to be protected within busy work programmes. Long-term strategies of nurturing potentially useful relationships are more difficult to justify and yet they are just as necessary because these informal, somewhat serendipitous, connections provide vital channels for information, resources and energy to flow through the circuits of civil society, linking community groups, local government politicians and officers, funding bodies and the array of voluntary organisations (Taylor, 1998). However, there are clearly limits to the amount of time community workers can spend simply tending relationships. Managers and funders expect outcomes and often need these delivered across a range of issues and within a given timescale.

Job constraints necessitate a division of labour and it is useful to keep strategic links with a variety of networks in order to stay in touch with areas of policy where direct involvement is limited or precluded. In some situations, the worker's identity (as perceived by others) may be a block to forming relationships, especially if differences in status or culture are involved. The characteristics and capabilities of the community worker may be a factor in negotiating access to certain communities or self-organising groups, such as specific ethnic populations. There is no reason why alternative means of staying abreast of developments in these groups cannot be found in order to gain up-to-date information and expertise around relevant issues, such as newsletters, television programmes or attendance at events as a supporter. Preparation is helpful because the more that is known and understood about the other people (their role, their interests, their background, the context in which they operate), the easier it is to find connections and to avoid causing offence or embarrassment. In many ways the competent networker will use the skills and quality of a good host at a large party: making people welcome, drawing them into conversation and introducing them to others who they might find compatible or stimulating. Good networking should be neither too blatant, nor overly focused. It is about facilitating interaction, helping people to make useful contacts and supporting the processes of relationship formation. Brokering and interpreting are important aspects of this.

Addressing inequalities

Major issues arise around power and dependency in relation to networking activities. All too often strategic and decision-making networks simply reflect and preserve current privileges, perpetuating inequalities and social exclusion (Hastings et al, 1996; Skelcher et al, 1996). An important role for the community worker is to expose and challenge semi-covert 'wheeling and dealing' by cliques operating in the corridors (or more usually pubs) of power. Good practice involves transparency, integrity and inclusion – working towards the wider benefit of the 'target' community or area. Community development's commitment to empowerment means that effective networking must span institutional boundaries and counter discrimination within organisations and communities. Dominance by professionals can present a problem, especially in situations where the pace of change is prescribed by external factors, such as funding programmes or performance criteria. Community development usually operates within political systems where workers can be persuasive either because of their position in the networks or because of their professional status. Practitioners must acknowledge their own influence while working to reduce power differentials.

> "What you're trying to do is to build up the ability of local people, the organisations that they create to shape their lives as much as possible ... the process is in some ways more important than the outcomes. It's never one thing or another. A process is pointless if it isn't generating outcomes but in a way it's more important to get the process right." (MW)

For a profession that asserts that participation should be open and equal, it might seem strange, even heretical, to promote networking as a core method of community development. Networking itself is a neutral tool and can have 'good' or 'bad' consequences, depending on circumstance and motivation. It needs to receive better recognition within community development practice and be underpinned by the values and commitments set out in Chapter Two.

Networking can lead to new projects and support systems being set up that offer a more formal means of challenging oppression and raising consciousness.

> "It puts people in touch with each other. I know for instance, my friend who started going to African history lessons ... is now sitting on a steering group with quite a few of her brothers and sisters who went to the same class as her, and they are now managing the African Young Men's steering group. I know a lot of them attended and began their African-centred learning at the same time. So I think that they chose to do something of personal interest [and] became a network which is ... now steering a project to really start to take action on African young men's issues in society." (SM)

Time for reciprocity

There needs to be greater acknowledgement by managers and funders that effective networking involves reciprocity – you have to *give* in order to *get*, and these informal gifts and favours are an investment for unpredictable future return. Helping out another organisation with a temporary problem, taking a turn to do the minutes of a meeting, offering advice or a sympathetic ear to a colleague, 'lending' the use of a meeting room or photocopying facilities – all detract from one's own work in the short-term, but lay a longer-term foundation in relationships of mutual support, respect and trust. The benefits of this work for the individual or the organisation rarely register in balance sheets or records of achievement, and yet are valuable contributions to community development. The costs of networking are often invisible or absorbed by a few individuals. They need to be recognised and shared more fairly, with attention paid to gender and role issues. This is important not only on grounds of equity, but also to ensure that power (administrative and emotional) does not accumulate to a small, unrepresentative clique. Time is needed to establish credibility and to develop a mental map of the various community and social networks. This may stretch over several years, often through a number of successive or overlapping jobs. Good networkers are recognised as a stable feature of the social and professional environment, operating as a 'rock' during times of upheaval, a 'fulcrum', a 'fountain' of useful information, the 'key link' between separate networks.

Networking takes time, and time to network has become an increasingly scarce commodity for practitioners faced with a need to meet targets and deadlines.

> "Giving time is a very valuable thing. But you've got to be strong to do it. To hold out against all the pressures not to do that and try and keep an eye

on the overall plan, but when it's really appropriate being able to make a critical judgement, [that] this person needs the time." (KT)

Short-term funding for projects being 'parachuted' into areas from national agencies and increasing emphasis on performance criteria can result in less efficient inter-agency working, strained relationships, frustration and a growing sense of isolation. Networking has been insufficiently supported or recognised, and often relies on the dedication of individuals either by default or because they have a particular talent or inclination. Greater recognition of this role would justify the flexibility and looser accountability of generic community development posts in local development agencies or intermediary bodies. Networking rarely has palpable or attributable 'outputs' and, consequently, funders and managers often do not appreciate its value.

> "It's quite difficult to justify the fact that networking is an efficient way of achieving something, because a lot of people don't think it is; a lot of people think it's just chatting and wasting time." (TD)

There has been a lack of investment in long-term generic community development that would allow workers to build up and maintain their contacts in an area. As a result, spontaneity and flexibility has been 'squeezed out' of many community development activities. This clearly has an impact on community workers' capacity to respond sensitively and strategically to needs and aspirations arising from community members, either collectively or as individuals. Community workers should be encouraged to experiment, to take risks and invest time in building up relationships within the community and with colleagues in organisations that they are likely to be working with. Giving time is an expression of commitment and respect. This should be acknowledged as 'work' even if it does not appear to have immediate or tangible outcomes.

Monitoring and evaluation

Networking interactions are often informal and happenstance. The connections set up are so delicate that they are sometimes not even recognised as such and are barely noted. Attempts to monitor and evaluate are clumsy by comparison, especially where they detect only predetermined performance criteria or quantifiable measures. Nevertheless it is important to review which sets of linkages may need strengthening or repairing, and which might be allowed to lapse or lie fallow for a while. The network map needs constantly updating in the light of changes to organisations, policies or personnel. The essence of 'good' networking lies in balanced and recurrent interaction, rather than transitory and purely instrumental contact. Most forms of evaluation fail to acknowledge the 'serendipity' effect in community work, namely that many perfectly useful and decent outcomes are not planned, nor even sometimes imagined. They appear instead from a fortuitous synchronicity to be found in everyday interactions (Cohen and Stewart, 1994). The challenge of monitoring and evaluating the effectiveness of networks is beginning to be addressed, for example in Skinner and Wilson's (2002) guide to assessing community strengths, but more evidence is needed on whether there is an optimal level of connectivity (equivalent to the 'edge of chaos') to be achieved by nurturing community networks. Some versions of 'social capital' emphasise the importance of networks over norms of trust, but this approach has not yet generated useful methods of measurement. Possibilities emerge from the concept of 'network capital' propounded by the Toronto school of network analysis (Sik and Wellman, 1999; Wellman, 2000). The New Economics Foundation is beginning to explore this approach to evaluating renewal programmes, in particular identifying the 'liveability' benefits to communities of growing trust and new, diverse connections formed through participation in local projects (Lingayah, 2001). Action research is needed to see how techniques of network analysis might sensibly be applied to community development.

Derricourt and Dale (1994, pp 84-5) suggest a 'matrix' form of evaluation that could be used to track changing agendas and alliances in an "unpredictable arena" of shifting loyalties and identities. Unfortunately, rigid procedures can discourage innovation and risk taking. It is rarely possible to predict the exact outcomes of community development, and in any case the requirement to do so stifles the initiative and synergy which networking generates. In the past community development work has been reluctant to demonstrate (and claim) its effectiveness in tackling problems and achieving results. As a profession, there has been an overemphasis on 'process' rather than product and it is right that this apparent lack of accountability has been challenged (Erskine and Breitenbach, 1994). It should be possible to develop evaluation frameworks that capture the hidden benefits of networking. The 'ABCD' approach first developed in Northern Ireland (Barr and Hashagen, 2000) provides a realistic and credible model for evaluating community development interventions, identifying informal networks as an important feature of community life:

> As well as tangible assets, communities are in one sense a sum of interpersonal and inter-group relationships. In a well-functioning community these will be well established and functional and a crucial part of how the community actually works. (Barr and Hashagen, 2000, p 56)

The benefits of networking should be viewed over the long-term, but networking without eventual outcomes can also be criticised. At some stage there have to be results in terms of things actually happening – new projects, proposals agreed, funding secured, and so on. The less visible improvements should also be recognised, such as increased cooperation among agencies, better representation on forums or consultative bodies, and more subtle changes in relationships and attitudes.

"The things that I try to get done can't get done unless people invested personal commitments in that, so they're proof of whether networks have come alive, or whether things have been done well.... In the course of achieving the different practical results you do kind of note whether there are shifts in the tone of relationships between yourself and other people." (MW)

Community workers know their networking to be effective when they are in demand. Other people hear of their work and they are invited to contribute to joint initiatives, their suggestions are taken up and implemented, they are used by others as an information resource and as a point of access into other networks.

"People say directly to you things like 'you've got an amazing network' ... or, more to the point (the real test of it), they send other people, particularly new people, new workers coming into the borough. I get a constant stream of them coming to me ... you do feel a sense of being appreciated. That's the main thing that indicates that I'm there as a resource person." (GrS)

Acquisition of networking capability

As we saw in Chapter Five, networking requires high levels of intuition. Some people feel that it involves skills that cannot be taught through formal training, but must be learnt through experience. In this respect the community worker can be seen as a significant role model for community activists. Studies of professional competence emphasise the artistic and intuitive aspects of professional practice that are evident in an ability to deal with complex and dynamic problems in "situations of uncertainty, instability, uniqueness and value conflict" (Schön, 1990, p 49).

"Maybe it stems right the way back as to how you were brought up in the first place ... in the sense that you accept people for what they are, you're no better or worse than anybody else, that we're all there to help each other ... maybe there's that in the background that comes over to other people." (LM)

Training in feeling and expressing empathy has been suggested as a way of enhancing attention and sensitivity to other people's feelings (Perlman, 1979, p 58; Egan, 1986). Similarly, being immersed in collective activities is a chance to learn skills in organising, communication and social interaction. In the Panel Study, community workers referred to adults, especially female relatives, as important role models. Kinship or community networks were described that provided a stable background in which trust, diversity and a sense of community were key components. Most of the Panel thought that their capacity to network was based on a subconscious 'inclination' or predisposition, rather than requiring specific knowledge and skills. And yet there was also a feeling that networking was a 'trick of the trade', a knack which *could* be acquired through experience or training. Adult behaviours and attitudes are acquired through experience, especially the social environment provided by our relationships with other people. This may be about developing social trust for, as Coulson observes, "trust is a process of learning. It grows through use ... and eventually it may reach a point where it is a matter of intuition and instinct" (1998, p 32). Early childhood shapes our 'personalities' through a process of socialisation – observation, action and selective reinforcement. We acquire those attitudes and abilities that are rewarded, and we seek out or create situations where we can exhibit behaviours that gain approval and tangible benefits. However, by understanding these influences and identifying traits that seem to support good networking, it is possible to adopt attitudes that make it easier to develop links with others and to be clearer about how to present one's 'self' in different arenas (cf Goffman, 1959). It is probable that anyone who is willing to put in time and effort, as well as listen to feedback from others, can improve their networking skills.

Women may have some advantage here due to upbringing and social status. There is evidence that women may think in more fluid and lateral ways, compared to men, making more effective use of intuition and inductive logic (Belenky, 1986). Gilligan (1982) suggests that this is particularly relevant to understanding gender differences in the skills and strategies that are used to manage social situations. She argues that girls learn patience, awareness of others' needs and relationship skills through childhood games that emphasise cooperation and role playing. As a result women have "developed the foundations of extremely valuable psychological qualities" (Miller, 1976, p 27), including enhanced abilities in non-verbal communication and emotional perception (Hall, 1984). In addition, adults tend to praise girls for being kind and thoughtful, while boys are rewarded for behaviour that is brave and independent. These differences become internalised as 'feminine' and 'masculine' characteristics and translated in later life into gendered roles, styles of working and moral frameworks. These tendencies are not genetically determined and it would be invidious to over-generalise but evidence, including the findings from the Panel Study, supports the observation that men are more achievement-oriented, more instrumentalist, while women tend to see themselves as responsible for managing relationships through the expression of care and attention towards others. The suspicion that women are more diligent and proficient networkers raises issues about how the outcomes of this work are acknowledged (and rewarded), because evaluation schemes often emphasise measurable performance targets and overlook the underlying processes that have contributed to their achievement. Skill and effort underpin effective networking, and it should be celebrated as valuable, but hitherto neglected 'women's work' developing 'community' and building social capital (Seron and Ferris, 1995; Blaxter et al, 2003).

Tensions and transitions

Networks provide extremely effective modes of organising and communicating in situations that are complex and uncertain, but they can also be muddled, biased and fragile. A lack of clarity over remits and responsibilities can cause problems when there is much work to be done or competition for scarce resources. This can lead to the kind of rivalry, mistrust and recriminations that beset those voluntary organisations that are overly reliant on trust and assumed common values (Beres and Wilson, 1997). Networks often have no organisational mechanisms for resolving disagreements among the contributors and this can be problematic when everyone is under pressure and nobody is willing to take a lead. Networks are sometimes expected to perform functions for which they are ill-suited, such as delivering services, or managing staff and resources. A culture of flexible and informal decision making is excellent for reaching people 'on the edge' and encouraging them to organise events or participate in community activities. Loose structures and informal methods of organising facilitate the flow of ideas and enable relatively disparate initiatives to emerge. Networks allow 'wild' ideas and tentative expressions of interest to crystallise into something more tangible. But for this to have a wider impact it needs coordinating, moulding into a collective demand or aspiration. Faith and favours are fine up to a point but they are not sufficient when organisational demands exceed resources, nor when there are competing external pressures and internal disagreements. Networks support organisation, but more formal procedures are needed for decision making and unified, rather than parallel, action (Jessop, 1997). This is not always recognised and tensions appear within networks when it appears that conventions or expectations are being violated, even though these are rarely made explicit. Community workers need to be aware of when networks might need to make this transition and be prepared to offer advice about how to establish more appropriate structures and procedures. This shift from informal network to formal organisation needs to be carefully handled and fully acknowledged by all concerned. Ideally, the new organisation should be set up to manage formal functions while leaving the networking capacity intact, but in reality this is not always possible.

Organisation development is an important aspect of community development and it would be useful to enhance our understanding of the evolutionary processes of informal groups and networks, perhaps looking at the optimal relationships between size, form and purpose. Morgan (1989, p 162) suggests that networks are manageable only up to the limits of personal engagement and surveillance, and I have accumulated ample anecdotal and empirical evidence that networks function best at around 35-40 participating members. This observation may reflect a trade-off between the costs of maintaining this number of links, and the benefits of their diverse contributions to voluntary collective action (cf McPherson, 1983, 1988). Computer simulations of networked systems also indicate that excessive connectivity can be a problem, reducing the adaptability of the whole system (Mulgan, 1997, p 186). This has implications for computer-mediated networking and suggests that within community development, direct networking between individuals has to be tempered by some degree of formal structure, to avoid information overload and the danger of tipping a system into chaos.

The impact of technology

Laslett (1956) was among the first to identify the importance of face-to-face communication in the creation of social groups capable of making collective decisions. In-person contact is a major component of networking because it allows the 'hidden dimension' (Hall, 1966) of non-verbal communication to function: managing first impressions, exerting subtle forms of influence, interpreting responses and regulating the pace and level of interaction (Patterson, 1991; Nohria and Eccles, 1992), especially in the initial phase of relationship building (Cole, 1997). It has been estimated that non-verbal communication conveys at least two thirds of the message, particularly when this is emotionally ambiguous or highly charged (Burgoon, 1981; Dunbar, 1996). Studies of human interactions emphasise the importance of para-linguistics (such as body language, posture, tone of voice) in regulating relationships (for example, Duck, 1992, p 75). This recognition has influenced the design of buildings, office layout and organisational structures (Hastings, 1993), but tends to be overlooked by the current enthusiasm for computer-mediated communication, possibly to the long-term detriment of 'real' community connections.

Recent developments in computer-based technologies have added a new (and somewhat contentious) dimension to the debate on community (Stone, 1991; Gordon, 1999; Chayko, 2002), raising issues around personal authenticity, access and accountability (Rheingold, 1993; Jones, 1995; Schuler, 1996). Technology certainly appears to facilitate information flow and connection across the 'digital society', but can this replicate (or even replace) the emotional basis of face-to-face interaction that constitutes genuine 'community' (Harris, 2003)? On the other hand, there is a plausible argument that services provided through the Internet (e-mailing, teleworking, surfing, shopping, virtual chatrooms and the like) actually improve communication, releasing time for relationships and serendipitous interactions within the neighbourhood and civil society (Mitchell, 1999; Watt et al, 2002). The impact of cyber-society and virtual networks on our lives is only beginning to be assessed empirically although studies of the use of computers to coordinate social and community activities are producing some interesting and encouraging findings (Wellman, and Guilia, 1999; Wellman and Haythornthwaite, 2002; Hampton, 2003).

Conclusions

This chapter has explored some of the challenges associated with a networking approach to community development. As practitioners, people working with communities need to be aware of the complexities and ambiguities in the community development role, and be prepared to manage their personal and professional networks in ways that promote cohesion, participation and empowerment. Issues around power, equality and diversity need to be constantly addressed in order that communities themselves develop the connections, capacity and confidence to maintain, extend and use networks to negotiate their own tensions and to have an influence over decisions that affect their circumstances and choices. Being 'well-connected' can only be an advantage in today's complex but unequal society.

NINE

Developing the well-connected community

'Only connect'. That was the sum total of her sermon. (E.M. Forster, 1910)

Community development as meta-networking

The complexity model of community development suggests that an important outcome of the community worker's interventions is being overlooked – namely the extent to which community networks are strengthened and diversified. As indicated earlier, community development can be reconceptualised as 'meta-networking': the coordination of interpersonal and interorganisational relationships within complex systems of interaction (Gilchrist, 1999). Community workers perform an undervalued function in facilitating interdisciplinary and cross-sectoral partnerships, with a particular role in identifying and supporting community members to work with others around shared issues and goals.

The community worker frequently provides the boundary-spanning link, the person who is able to operate within different settings and constituencies acting as broker or interpreter, especially at times of misunderstanding or conflict. The community worker has a crucial role in 'networking the networks'. They spin and mend connections across the web: putting people in touch with one another, helping them to communicate effectively and generally supporting the more difficult links, the ones blocked by organisational barriers, misunderstandings or prejudice. They may simply operate as a 'go-between', keeping the pathway open as a route for future cooperation. The community worker often acts as an important node in community and cross-sectoral networks: a source of information which others can use to make connections or to find support.

Networking is of intrinsic benefit to community development practice and to communities. Although it may prove impossible to 'proceduralise networking' (Hosking and Morley, 1991, p 224), the Panel Study identified specific strategies and outcomes which were achieved through networking. A model of 'good networking practice' is proposed that draws together the experiences of practitioners' Panel and the Festival Against Racism. This includes recommendations for community work as an occupation in terms of core principles, role management, training and support structures. It may be helpful to summarise the key recommendations (see Table 6) before going on to explain why they are important.

Table 6: Summary of key recommendations for policy and practice

Recommendation	Explanation
1. Networking should be explicitly acknowledged as a core activity within community development practice	It should be included in job descriptions, person specifications, work programmes and funding applications
2. Networking should be better monitored and managed through work reports, which identify informal interaction with key or new contacts as well as formal inter-organisational liaison	An index of effective networking practice could include criteria for performance appraisal. This could incorporate short-term impact measures, as well as longer-term outcomes
3. The meta-networking aspect of generic community work should be incorporated into employment conditions through long-term contracts with secure funding	Supervision and training should be available to community workers (and others) to improve their networking abilities, and to recognise the difficulties and dilemmas inherent in networking approaches
4. The less tangible aspects of human interaction derived from intuition and informal networking should be recognised and valued as important ways of working with people to develop collective action and multi-agency initiatives	Greater flexibility in work programmes allows for experimentation and unexpected developments that emerge as a result of networking activities
5. The importance of networking as a foundation for partnership arrangements needs to be recognised in the timescales for developing bids, delivery plans and formal management structures	Partners need time together to develop a shared vision, to build trust, to deal with disagreements and to address power differentials. Team-building exercises may help, as will informal social activities
6. A code of good practice in networking may need to be established setting out ethical standards	This should cover issues around role boundaries, reciprocity, accountability, confidentiality, equal opportunities and covert influence
7. Opportunities for informal networking should be included (and sometimes facilitated) within formal events, such as conferences, training courses or inter-agency meetings	A balance is needed between structured time at events, and time when participants can make contact and informally follow up discussions with one another
8. The function of intermediary bodies in helping community and voluntary organisations to develop cooperative and 'learningful' connections across identity and geographic boundaries should be strengthened	Umbrella bodies, such as Councils for Voluntary Service or specialist forums, provide vital opportunities for information exchange and debate across the whole sector and need support to make sure their facilities are accessible to all sections of the sector
9. Techniques of network analysis could provide a baseline 'snapshot' of how communities are operating	This could provide a good opportunity for participatory appraisal research involving community members
10. Evaluation of community development programmes should include outcomes, which relate to improved relationships and connections within communities, and between communities and organisations in other sectors	Longitudinal network mapping exercises should indicate how the linkages between groups and organisations within communities change as a result of community development interventions and show in graphic form any isolated clusters and gaps in communication

Networking for better practice

Networking enhances the quality of community development and service delivery generally. The morale and knowledge of individual staff is improved because practitioners become more reflective and benefit from critical discussion with colleagues, developing a sharper analysis of their work. Informal comparisons and debate encourage people to keep their ideas fresh, to stay informed, to review their work, to maintain key values and principles and to challenge poor standards and complacency. This is how 'best practice' can be consolidated and examined, so that theories can be developed as to why some approaches seem to work better than others. Networks are a source of friendly support that recognise and reinforce commitment to the job, without which many community development practitioners would become isolated and discouraged. Networking with other community workers or like-minded people creates opportunities for informal support, supervision, advice and mentoring. Panelists used their networks to examine the validity of their own ideas and to consider alternative perspectives. Networks provide a useful 'sounding board' at moments of crisis and an occasional shoulder to cry on. Community development practitioners survive through their peer networks (Ingamells, 1996). Feedback from informal mentors and trusted allies is an important source of constructive criticism, enabling people to correct and adjust their behaviour accordingly. Informal networking creates 'safe' and supportive environments where practitioners can talk things through with like-minded colleagues. They are able to explore contentious issues, upgrade their professional skills and knowledge and reflect critically on their own practice. In the absence of formal supervision arrangements and in-service training, this form of peer education enables community workers (who are often in lone or peripheral posts), to cope with stress and to manage what are often quite complicated work programmes. As we saw in Chapter One, the social support provided by personal relationships can be crucial to survival, job satisfaction and success, helping people to cope in environments that are unfamiliar, precarious or downright hostile. Networking helps community development workers to face similar situations, especially in settings where funding is uncertain or misunderstandings abound about the nature of the job.

It is clear from the Panel Study and the practice literature that professional community development involves proficient, sometimes expert networking, requiring intelligence, ingenuity and intuition. It takes time and effort in terms of self-presentation, preparation and discovering the 'lay of the land'. Effective networking is skilled, strategic and sustainable. It can be improved through reflection, practice and experience. Networking involves two layers of competence. The first refers to the maintenance of relationships between the worker and others. The second aspect, here termed 'meta-networking' is about supporting and shaping the web of connections that weaves across the communities and links them into the wider world. Meta-networking involves the usual skills and processes of networking such as making contact, finding connections, crossing boundaries, building relationships and interpersonal communication. It also requires an ability to manage the resultant network of relationships as a resource which others can make use of. This is difficult because the links themselves are multi-faceted and delicate, while the web as a whole comprises a complex system of intricate connections.

It is possible to increase people's capacity to network by improving skills, knowledge and motivation. An Internet search for material on 'community networks' invariably generates copious references to information technology and there are plenty of guidance manuals on the use of computers to capture, compare and communicate all kinds of data (Lipnack and Stamps, 1994). This privileging of technological networking over human interaction is a worrying but salutary reminder that knowledge management is an essential function of networking. Knowledge management is about enabling people collectively to share and apply knowledge so that they can achieve their respective goals and objectives. To be effective, the successful networker needs to be able to acquire, assimilate and access information, preferably in a form that will benefit those who might need it most. This requires good administrative and organisational skills, notably some kind of system for storing and retrieving information. This might be an excellent memory, but it may also be wise to use notes, a computer database, or all three.

Knowledge management is not simply about the dissemination of information. Community development workers analyse, interpret, evaluate and synthesise ideas from an extraordinary range of sources. This deluge of information includes official statistics, gossip, rumour, policy statements, ideological dogma, legal documents, political demands, cries for help, dreams, aspirations, half-remembered impressions and formal reports. The effective networker is able, somehow, to make sense of this kaleidoscope of inconsistent and incomplete versions of the world, assemble some kind of coherent assessment and then present this for others to consider. This requires complex cognitive processes by which patterns and congruencies are identified amid apparently contradictory opinions, facts and beliefs. Community development workers use their networks to develop insights into situations. They should be able to fairly and accurately present opposing views and make sensible forecasts of future developments based on their knowledge of past and current events. The good networker must therefore develop and exercise a political analysis of situations, taking into account power dynamics and personal interests, alongside their own ideologies and status.

Adaptable communication skills are needed so that the community worker can understand and interpret key messages across cultural and institutional boundaries. People from different organisations and communities think in different ways and may use language differently, including non-verbal forms of communication. It is therefore important to understand how body language carries different significance in different settings and cultures, and to act accordingly. Good networkers need to be alert to potential misunderstandings and anticipate friction among people from different backgrounds, whether this is about working with people from different sectors or from different parts of the world. It is useful to have an understanding of the diverse conventions and traditions that may influence people's behaviour in complex social or organisational environments (Hopkins, 1997). An important component of networking capacity is an overview of the environment in which one is operating, including an up-to-date 'map' of the organisational field (and the relationships that weave across it). Network mapping exercises enable people to be more aware of existing links among organisations, and more explicit about how they use (or could use) connections with other individuals or agencies. By identifying actual and potential forms of cooperation, it is suggested that people can become more proactive, and consequently more effective, in their networking. Organisational diagrams are helpful in conflict situations because they encourage participants to interrogate (and adjust) the network arrangements rather than antagonise each other (Taket and White, 1997). Similarly power mapping has been used in developing countries and in the UK to trace and where possible 'unscramble' divergent interests (Estrella and Gaventa, 1998; Mayo and Taylor, 2001). Understanding how the people one is working with are connected (or not) and how this affects the organisation of collective activities is crucial to all successful community development strategies. Computer simulations, network analysis and visualisation programmes are currently being developed to promote, manage and evaluate organisational change, but have not yet been systematically applied to community development (Freeman et al, 1998).

Practical manuals on networking have been published (McCabe et al, 1997; LGMB, 1998) and several guides or training packs have been recently produced to improve people's strategic and technical capabilities (for example, Lyford, 2001; WCAN, 2002; SCCD, 2003). The ability to develop and maintain relationships with a *range* of people, and to communicate in a *variety* of modes is given insufficient recognition as a necessary competence and this could easily be improved by encouraging community workers to gain experience in a wider range of practice situations than is currently the norm. Motivation is an important factor and most good networkers seem to possess a genuine curiosity in other people and other cultures, as well as an understanding that fostering good relationships will help them in their community development work.

Intermediary bodies and partnership working

Since networking clearly takes time, effort and attention, this work needs to be recognised and adequately funded if community development and partnership working is to be effective and sustainable. Core funding for long-term generic community work posts would be helpful, allowing workers to understand and engage with community dynamics, build meaningful relationships and respond to issues identified by community members themselves. As Taylor (1995b) and others have demonstrated, the ability of residents to become and stay involved with regeneration programmes is developed through long experience of collective organising. Community participation and collective empowerment emerge from a complex infrastructure of informal networks and self-organising groups. It is this layer of interaction which is neglected by, and yet essential to the recent successes in community-led regeneration programmes (Stewart, 1998). It needs to be supported both by generic community work posts and by adequately funded, but independent, umbrella bodies. It may seem obvious that the existence of 'community' is a prerequisite for community involvement, and yet few policy officers or regeneration managers realise that key elements of community capacity – networks, interaction, common purpose, collective identity and organisational infrastructure – may need to be in place *before* there can be effective and equal partnership.

Government policy under New Labour has been strongly influenced by communitarian thinking and a commitment to subsidiarity. There has been a return to ideas of community participation in decision making based on collective empowerment rather than individualist 'user' or consumer rights. There has been further emphasis on partnership and 'joined-up' working, accompanied by a growing understanding that this requires 'capacity building'. While there is still a tendency to assume that the deficit lies with local residents rather than officers and representatives of the private and statutory partners, there is growing evidence that shared capacity-building programmes (where all partners train together) are most effective in promoting learning and trust (Scott et al, 2002). Without commitment and clarity around the *practice* of partnerships and devolution, there is a danger that independent community initiatives will be subsumed into a rather top-down approach which delivers to the government's modernising agenda rather than pursuing community priorities (Burgess et al, 2001).

Community initiatives and processes are organic, needing space and support to grow. Voluntary sector 'umbrella' bodies provide both the trellising and the nutrients for this growth, but have been under threat from local authority funding cuts and from the appearance of agencies with a more specialist function, for example, supporting volunteering, delivering services or encouraging social enterprise. Intermediary bodies often act as social relays and brokers, enabling smaller organisations to network with one another and connecting informal networks into more formal partnerships (Skelcher et al, 1996; Taylor, 1997). Many intermediary bodies perform a coordinating function: convening meetings, producing mailings, running training workshops, providing specific advice and facilitating consultation exercises. Local forums, federations and network bodies provide a similar service, sometimes with paid administrative support, but more often reliant on the dedication of a few hard-pressed individuals who are able (just about) to undertake these tasks on top of other work commitments.

Studies of multi-agency partnership working (Goss and Kent, 1995; Hambleton et al, 1995; Stewart and Taylor, 1995; Means et al, 1997; Geddes, 1998) invariably found relationships and informal networks to have a major (and not always positive) impact on the quality of decision making and cooperation. Partnerships tend to involve prominent and 'well-connected' key players: community leaders, voluntary sector professionals or local authority officers who are able to influence decisions through their contacts with politicians and funders. Access to such networks is rarely either transparent or equitable, and can be a major source of resentment and discrimination. This unevenness in networking capacity is being addressed through government grants attached to the neighbourhood renewal programme that allocate funding specifically to set up 'community empowerment networks' so that communities can be better represented on strategic partnerships.

Community involvement in government initiatives depends on a foundation of community sector activity that is low profile, but somehow enduring over time (Chanan, 1999). Supporting this layer of active citizenship, self-help and mutuality is a core function of community development, which should be better supported by government (Burns and Taylor, 1998). The National Strategy for Neighbourhood Renewal asserts that "thriving communities are those which interact with their surroundings", suggesting that community activity (or volunteering as it is termed here) "brings people into contact with those outside their normal circles, broadening horizons and raising expectations, and can link people into informal networks" (SEU, 2000, Section 6.3). In addition to organised activities, chapter 6 on 'Reviving Communities' argues for facilities, such as neighbourhood shops and multi-purpose venues, which encourage informal contact between residents. This focus on local space is welcome, but sometimes, interaction requires a more proactive approach to overcome shyness, unfamiliarity or prejudices, encouraging people to get to know one another rather than simply pass on the streets. Funding policies need to secure existing good practice at community level, including money for positive action measures, such as crèches, the provision of interpreters and personal assistance for Disabled people. The tendency for grant-giving bodies to support only new or innovative projects has distorted community work practice and undermined the basis for creative thinking and genuine community participation. There are signs that government policy is recognising the value of long-term interventions in building the 'capacity' of communities to engage with regeneration and renewal programmes. Recent reviews conducted by the Home Office have focused on improving the infrastructure of the voluntary and community sectors (ACU, 2003; CRU, 2003). There appears to be an increased willingness among politicians and policy makers to trust agencies and professions that are not under their immediate control, and to acknowledge that risk, discretion and occasional failure are inevitable corollaries of pursuing strategies which urge community enterprise and innovation. If these approaches are to be successful, community development needs space and opportunity for informal and serendipitous activities to operate alongside more formal task-related projects. Global and social changes suggest that:

The future for work which links the neighbourhood to the wider world is likely to lie in looser and more flexible networks ... but issues of transparency, accountability and access will need to be addressed if these networks are to be grounded in the needs of people in communities and in acknowledged democratic processes.... It is likely that in a more fragmented 'post-modern' environment, networks and alliances will be the foundation on which empowerment is built. Community workers need to develop a practice which can work with allies across the institutional map to find the possibilities for change in an increasingly turbulent environment. (Taylor, 1995a, pp 109–10)

A new paradigm for sustainability

The current buzz terms of 'sustainability' and 'liveability' reflect two linked policy agendas. On the one hand, sustainable development refers to the integration of social, economic and environmental objectives within a single strategy or programme. It is about improving the quality of life by making sure that gains in one area of policy do not jeopardise the achievement of other goals. Sustainability is also concerned with ensuring the continuing effectiveness of regeneration and renewal interventions through changes to mainstream services. Informal networks create a foundation for effective collective action and the empowerment of disadvantaged communities. The networking approach to community development argues that a core function of practice is to help individuals and organisations to establish and make use of connections that reach across boundaries. Networking, therefore, is not an incidental or peripheral activity. It must become more strategic, more skilful, better managed and more realistically funded. Well-functioning, liveable communities need both weak and strong ties. The primary task of community development interventions is to set up and maintain the 'bridging' mechanisms, either through the networking activities of the community worker themselves or by supporting projects which create and sustain linkages between organisations and separate sections of the population (Barr et al, 1997; Taylor 2000b, p 1027). This is particularly important for oppressed and minority groups where resources are limited and yet there is an urgent need to influence policy (Qaiyoom, 1992). A networking approach strengthens the informal infrastructure of communities, so that relationships develop between members of different groups. It is vital to provide channels for marginalised and dissenting voices to be heard and create cross-cutting forums that encourage discussion, democratic decision making and collective problem solving (Wittenbaum and Stasser, 1996). The boundary-spanning aspects of informal networks are crucial in creating a climate for learning and innovation. Weak ties contribute to social cohesion by providing links between sections of the networks that might otherwise remain isolated and mutually antagonistic (Granovetter, 1978). Strong ties, characterising intimate kin and friendship clusters, where members are connected through many overlapping links, provide multiple communication channels, and this internal redundancy gives communities their resilience. If one relationship fails or becomes overloaded, there are several other possible information routes or sources of support.

Community development is fundamentally concerned with long-term change. Butcher (1993, p 17) see the 'end product' of community practice as a "neighbourhood alive with activity and cross-cut with networks of relationships, providing a locus for informal support and mutual aid", to which might be added 'and for collective organising'. In many respects, the model of the 'well-connected community' presented in this book was pre-empted over a decade ago by Flecknoe and McLellan who recognised in their introduction to neighbourhood work that:

> The community development process sets out to create the context within which meaningful relationships can be formed and through which people have the spaces to grow and change, and fulfil their potential.... A high quality of relationships is the foundation for all community development work. Unless people are able to trust in others and share a part of their lives, collective activity is impossible.... 'Community' is that web of personal relationships, group networks, traditions and patterns of behaviour that develop against the backdrop of the physical neighbourhood and its socio-economic situation. Community development aims to enrich that web and make its threads stronger. (1994, pp 7-8)

Complexity theory provides an explanation of *why* networks form the basis for an optimally functioning social system. These can be characterised by mildly 'chaotic' interactions leading to the evolution of collective forms of organising that adapt or die according to changes in the social environment. The model of the 'well-connected community' sees 'community' as neither a place, nor an agent of change, nor even a 'fuzzy set' of characters. 'Community' is conceptualised as an experience or capacity that emerges as a result of the interactions within a complex web of overlapping networks (Wellman, 1999). The development of 'community' is an aspiration, a principle and an outcome. Managing the 'web' of interpersonal and interorganisational linkages is a vital professional function that acknowledges the diversity, the difficulties and the dynamism of communities, all important features of complex systems.

While it is true that a proportion of the work is conducted through one-to-one conversations, assistance and support, networking for community development is primarily about helping people to form connections that will be beneficial to them personally, to overcome psychological and other barriers and facilitate their participation in broader activities and decision making. Work with individuals is a necessary, but not sufficient contribution to the establishment and maintenance of groups, organisations and coalitions. Thomas (1995, p 15) refers to this as the 'lost meaning' of community development, the work that "strengthens the social resources and processes in a community by developing those *contacts, relationships, networks, agreements and activities* outside the household" (emphasis in original). The new paradigm set out in this book seeks to restore the value of this work by locating networking at the heart of community development.

It has been suggested that at least half the work in organisations is done through networks that are invisible to management (Stephenson, 1998). In the same way, collective action and partnership working rely on and are enhanced by largely unacknowledged networking. Much of this takes place informally through face-to-face conversation and mutual cooperation. An examination of the micro-practices of networking within community development reveals it to be skilled, strategic *and* serendipitous. It requires knowledge of local customs, organisational structures and cultural institutions, as well as a commitment to building trust and respect across community and sectoral boundaries, especially those relating to ethnicity, class and other dimensions of society. Networking offers an effective tool for honouring diversity, promoting equality and managing the tensions that arise from cultural differences.

Conclusions

The model of the 'well-connected community' and the idea of 'meta-networking' are presented here as a core purpose of community development practice. This is fundamentally about nurturing informal social, political and professional networks using informal links and organisational liaison to hold a 'community system' at the 'edge of chaos'. In his most recent consideration of the functioning of complex systems, Kauffman (2001) recognises that some kind of intervention is necessary to create 'order from chaos'. He suggests that this may involve a catalytic presence in the system or a sustained influx of energy (or both). In some circumstances, the commitment and connections supplied by community workers are crucial in helping the 'well-connected community' to adapt to changing conditions in its organisational and political environment. The community worker as meta-networker must be both strategic and opportunistic. They need to maintain a balance between the formal and informal aspects of community life, operating within a complex accountability matrix in a context that is shaped by political, cultural and psychological processes. As I have written elsewhere, they are both catalyst and connector (Gilchrist, 1998b).

The networking approach to community development opens up access and communication routes across the social and political landscape, exploiting personal habits, local conventions and institutional power in order to improve the quality of life for individuals and create mechanisms for collective empowerment. Complexity theory suggests that a community poised at the 'edge of chaos' is able to survive in 'turbulent times' because it evolves forms of collective organisations that fit the environmental conditions. If, as I am suggesting, meta-networking is a key professional function, then we need to find ways of evaluating community development in terms of improvements to interpersonal and interorganisational links within wider networks. This involves looking at the intricacy and effectiveness of the individual relationships (Parikh, 1999) as well as levels of diversity and 'connectedness' across the whole web, including interactions with the 'outside' world. Community indicators used in participatory appraisals that measure the feel-good factors of community life offer further possibilities (MacGillivray and Zadek, 1996; Walker et al, 2000), as do the relational audits suggested by the Relationship Foundation (Baker, 1996). Morrisey (2000) reports on an action research study to evaluate citizen participation and learning which included as progress indicators: 'development of new networks', 'levels of trust', 'alliances among organisations', 'organisations with networks formed', and (for individuals) 'expanded network of relationships' and 'learning the importance of networking'. In particular, it will be important to develop ways of assessing the robustness of networks and measuring the 'interconnectivity' between individuals and organisations (Skinner and Wilson, 2002, pp 152-4). More work is needed to establish the link between networking practice and community development outcomes, especially since the recent introduction of a local government power to promote 'social well-being' and a growing interest in measuring social capital (Boek and McCulloch, 2001; Putnam, 2001; Smyth, 2001; Halpern, 2004: forthcoming).

The 'well-connected community' model reconciles individual interests with the common good through the development of a 'reflexive imagination' and locally appropriate problem-solving strategies. Complexity theory encourages us to see informal and interorganisational networks as an extended communal 'brain', processing information intelligently to construct a resilient body of knowledge, and generating a collective consciousness at the same time (cf Morgan, 1986; Rose, 1998). As Wilson observes, "the brain is a machine assembled not to understand itself, but to survive.... The brain's true meaning is hidden in its microscopic detail. Its fluffy mass is an intricately wired system" (1998, p 106). By analogy the capacity of a community to respond creatively to change and ambiguity is to be found in its web of connections and relationships, rather than in either the heads of individuals or the formal structures of voluntary bodies. A well-connected community is able to solve problems through reasoning, experimentation and strategic engagement with external bodies, not just trial and error. The well-connected community will demonstrate insight and intelligence, responding to local or external perturbations and accommodating internal diversity. It will be capable of learning from experience and developing strategies for dealing with unusual situations and eventualities (Morgan, 1989; Capra, 1996). In the long run, community development offers a cost-effective and sustainable strategy for regenerating communities, and renewing civil society but it will need better understanding and more resources than are currently available.

The starting point for this book was a recognition that 'things' happened as a result of informal interactions even though these often failed to register in formal auditing, monitoring and evaluation procedures. Social relations and networks represent intangible resources in people's lives that can either be nurtured or allowed to wither through neglect. Networking ensures that personal and social capital are generated and maintained within communities. Community workers have a particular responsibility for the 'weak ties' that span socio-psychological boundaries, thus keeping open the channels of communication within and between diverse communities, promoting integration and building 'alliance across difference' (Mayo, 2000). In a world characterised by uncertainty and diversity, the networking approach enables people to make links across society, to share resources and learn from each other without the costs and constraints of formal organisational structures. Empowerment is a collective process, achieved through compassion, communication and connections. This book is a contribution to the discussion on how community development uses networking to develop 'community' and to promote 'strength through diversity'.

References

6, Perri (1997a) *Escaping poverty: From safety nets to networks of opportunity*, London: Demos.

6, Perri (1997b) *The power to bind and lose: Tackling network poverty*, London: Demos.

6, Perri (2002) 'Governing friends and acquaintances: public policy and social networks', in V. Nash (ed) *Reclaiming community*, London: IPPR.

Abrams, D. and Hogg, M.A. (1990) *Social identity theory*, Hemel Hempstead: Harvester Wheatsheaf.

Abrams, P. and McCulloch, A. (1976) *Communes, sociology and society*, Cambridge: Cambridge University Press.

ACU (Active Community Unit) (2003) *Voluntary and community sector infrastructure: A consultation document*, London: Home Office.

ACW (Association of Community Workers) (1975) *Knowledge and skills for community work*, London: ACW.

ACW (1978) *Conditions of employment for those working in the community: Guidance for workers and employers*, London: ACW.

Agranoff, R. and McGuire, M. (2001) 'Big questions in public network management research', *Journal of Public Administration Research and Theory*, vol 3, pp 295-326.

Ahrne, G. (1994) *Social organisations*, London: Sage Publications.

Albrecht, L. and Brewer, R.M. (1990) 'Bridges of power', in L. Albrecht and R.M. Brewer (eds) *Bridges of power: Women's multi-cultural alliances*, Philadelphia, PA: New Society.

Alinsky, S. (1969) *Reveille for radicals*, New York, NY: Vintage Books.

Alinsky, S. (1972) *Rules for radicals*, New York, NY: Vintage Books.

Allport, G. (1958) *The nature of prejudice*, New York, NY: Doubleday.

Allport, G.W. and Postman, L. (1947) *The psychology of rumour*, New York, NY: Henry Holt and Co.

Alperin, D. (1990) 'Social diversity and the necessity of alliances – a developing feminist perspective', in L. Albrecht and R.M. Brewer (eds) *Bridges of power: Women's multi-cultural alliances*, Philadelphia, PA: New Society.

AMA (Association of Metropolitan Authorities) (1993) *Local authorities and community development: A strategic opportunity for the 1990s*, London: AMA.

Amado, R. (1993) 'Loneliness: effects and implications', in R. Amado (ed) *Friendships and community connections between people with and without developmental disabilities*, Baltimore, MD: Paul H. Brookes.

Amin, A. and Hausner, J. (1997) 'Interactive governance and social complexity', in A. Amin and J. Hausner (eds) *Beyond market and hierarchy: Interactive governance and social complexity*, Cheltenham: Edward Elgar Publishing Ltd.

Anastacio, J., Gidley, B., Hart, L., Keith, M., Mayo, M. and Korwarzik, V. (2000) *Reflecting realities: Participants' perspectives on integrated communities and sustainable development*, Bristol/York: The Policy Press/Joseph Rowntree Foundation.

Anderson, B. (1983) *Imagined communities: Reflections on the origin and spread of nationalism*, London: Verso.

Anderson, J. (1995) *How to make an American quilt screenplay*, Los Angeles, CA: Universal City Studios.

Anthias, F. and Yuval-Davies, N. (1992) *Racialized boundaries: Race, nation, gender, colour and class and the anti-racist struggle*, London: Routledge.

Anwar, M. (1985) *Pakistanis in Britain: A sociological study*, London: New Century.

Anwar, M. (1995) 'Social networks of Pakistanis in the UK: a re-evaluation', in A. Rogers and S. Vertovec (eds) *The urban context*, Oxford/Washington, DC: Berg Publishers.

Appiah, K.A. (1999) *Globalising rights*, Oxford Amnesty Lecture, reported in *Oxford Today* magazine, Trinity [Summer].

Appleyard, D. (1981) *Liveable streets*, Berkeley, CA: University of California Press.

Argyle, M. (1989) *The psychology of happiness*, London: Routledge.

Argyle, M. (1996a) 'The effects of relationships on well-being', in N. Baker (ed) *Building a relational society: New priorities for public policy*, Aldershot: Arena.

Argyle, M. (1996b) *The social psychology of leisure*, Harmondsworth: Penguin.

Arrow, K.J. (1974) *The limits of organisation*, New York, NY: Norton.

Ayim, M. (1994) 'Knowledge through the grapevine: gossip as inquiry', in R.F. Goodman and A. Ben-Ze'ev (eds) *Good gossip*, Kansas, TX: University Press of Kansas.

Bachrach, P. and Baratz, M.S. (1962) 'Two faces of power', *American Political Science Review*, vol 56, pp 947-52.

Back, L. (1996) *New ethnicities and urban culture*, London: UCL Press.

Baddley, S. and James, K. (1987) 'From political neutrality to political wisdom', *Politics*, vol 7, no 2, pp 35-40.

Baine, S. (1974) 'The political community', in M. Mayo and D. Jones (eds) *Community work one*, London: Routledge and Kegan Paul.

Baker, N. (ed) (1996) *Building a relational society: New priorities for public policy*, Aldershot: Arena.

Baker, W. (1992) 'The network organisation in theory and practice', in N. Nohria and R.G. Eccles (eds) *Networks and organisations: Structure, form and action*, Boston, MA: Harvard Business School Press.

Baker, W. (1994) *Networking smart: How to build relationships for personal and organisational success*, New York, NY: McGraw-Hill.

Baldock, P. (1977) 'Why community action? The historical origins of the radical trend in British community work', *Community Development Journal*, vol 12, no 2, pp 68-74.

Ball, C. and Ball, M. (1982) *What the neighbours say*, Berkhamstead: The Volunteer Centre.

Banks, S., Butcher, H., Henderson, P. and Robertson, J. (eds) (2003) *Managing community practice: Principles, policies and programmes*, Bristol: The Policy Press.

Barclay, P. (1982) *Social workers: Their roles and tasks*, London: Bedford Square Press.

Barnett, R. (1994) *The limits of competence: Knowledge, higher education and society*, Buckingham: Open University Press.

Barnett, S.A. (1888) 'Charity up to date', in S. Barnett (ed) *Practicable socialism*, London: Longmans Green and Co.

Barnett, S.A. (1904) *Towards social reform*, London: T. Fisher and Unwin.

Baron, S., Field, J. and Schuller, T. (2000) *Social capital: Critical perspectives*, Oxford: Oxford University Press.

Barr, A. (1977) *The practice of neighbourhood community work*, Paper No 12 Community Studies series, York: University of York.

Barr, A. and Hashagen, S. (2000) *ABCD handbook: A framework for evaluating community development*, London: Community Development Foundation.

Barr, A., Drysdale, J. and Henderson, P. (1997) *Towards caring communities? Community development and community care*, Brighton: Pavilion.

Barton, A.H. (1969) *Communities in disaster: A sociological analysis of collective stress situations*, Garden City, NY: Doubleday.

Barton, H. (2000) 'The design of neighbourhoods', in H. Barton (ed) *Sustainable communities: The potential for eco-neighbourhoods*, London: Earthscan.

Barton, H., Grant, M. and Guise, S. (2002) *Shaping neighbourhoods: A guide for health, sustainability and vitality*, London: Spon Press.

Bassinet-Bourget, M.-R. (1991) 'Social networks: learning to work together', in W. van Rees (ed) *A survey of contemporary community development in Europe*, The Hague: Dr Gradus Hendriks-Stichting.

Batsleer, J. and Randall, S. (1992) 'Creating common cause', in J. Batsleer, C. Cornforth and R. Paton (eds) *Issues in voluntary and non-profit management*, Wokingham: Addison–Wesley.

Batten, T.R. (1957) *Communities and their development*, Oxford: Oxford University Press.

Batten, T.R. (1962) *Training for community development: A critical study of method*, London: Oxford University Press.

Batten, T.R. and Batten, M. (1967) *The non-directive approach in group and community work*, London: Oxford University Press.

Baum, F. (2000) 'Social capital, economic capital and power: further issues for a public health agenda', *Journal of Epidemiological Community Health*, vol 54, pp 409-10.

Bauman, Z. (1991) *Modernity and ambivalence*, Cambridge: Polity Press.

Bayley, M. (1997) 'Empowering and relationships', in P. Ramcharan (ed) *Empowerment in everyday life: Learning disability*, London: Jessica Kingsley.

Bechtel, W. and Abrahamsen, A. (1991) *Connectionism and the mind: An introduction to parallel processing in networks*, Oxford: Blackwell.

Belenky, M. (1986) *Women's way of knowing: The development of self, voice and mind*, New York, NY: Basic Books.

Bell, C. and Newby, H. (1971) 'Community studies, community power and community conflict', in C. Bell and C. Newby (eds) *Community studies*, London: George Allen and Unwin.

Bell, J. (1992) *Community development team work: Measuring the impact*, London: CDF.

Benington, J. (1998) 'Risk and reciprocity: local governance rooted within civil society', in A. Coulson (ed) *Trust and contracts: Relationships in local government, health and public services*, Bristol: The Policy Press.

Bennis, W.G. and Nanus, B. (1985) *Leaders: The strategies for taking charge*, New York, NY: Harper and Row.

Benson, J.K. (1975) 'The inter-organisational network as a political economy', *Administrative Science Quarterly*, vol 20, pp 229-49.

Beres, Z. and Wilson, G. (1997) 'Essential emotions: the place of passion in a feminist network', *Non-profit Management and Leadership*, vol 8, no 2, pp 171-82.

Beresford, P. (1993) 'Service users and networking', in S. Trevillion (ed) *Networking and community care: An anthropological perspective*, papers presented at the Networking and Community Care conference, November 1992, London: West London Institute, Brunel University.

Berger, P.L. (1997) *Redeeming laughter: The comic dimension of human experience*, New York, NY: de Gruyter.

Berry, C.J. (1984) *The idea of a democratic community*, Hemel Hempstead: Harvester Wheatsheaf.

Biddle, W.W. (1968) 'Deflating the community developer', *Community Development Journal*, vol 3, no 4, pp 191-4.

Biddle, W.W. and Biddle, L.J. (1965) *The community development process*, New York, NY: Holt, Rinehart and Winston.

Blane, D., Brimmer, E. and Wilkinson, R. (1996) *Health and social organisation: Towards a health policy for the 21st century*, London: Routledge.

Blaxter, L., Farnell, R. and Watts, J. (2003) 'Difference, ambiguity and the potential for learning – local communities working in partnership with local government', *Community Development Journal*, vol 38, no 2, pp 130-9.

Blunkett, D. (2001) *Politics and progress: Renewing democracy and civil society*, London: Demos, Politico's Publishing.

Boek, T. and McCulloch, P. (2001) *Social capital survey: Saffron lane estate*, Leicester: De Montfort University.

Böhm, D. (1994) *Thought as a system*, London: Routledge.

Boissevain, J. (1974) *Friends of friends: Networks, manipulators and coalitions*, Oxford: Blackwell.

Bott, E. (1957) *Family and social networks*, London: Tavistock.

Bourdieu, P. (1986) 'The forms of capital', in J.G. Richardson (ed) *Handbook of theory and research for the sociology of education*, New York, NY: Greenwood Press.

Bourke, J. (1994) *Working class cultures in Britain – 1890-1960*, London: Routledge.

Braddach, J.L. and Eccles, R.G. (1989) 'Price, authority and trust: from ideal types to plural forms', *Annual Review of Sociology*, vol 15, pp 97-118.

Bradshaw, T. (2000) 'Complex community development projects: collaboration, comprehensive programs and community coalitions in complex society', *Community Development Journal*, vol 35, no 2, pp 133-45.

Breakwell, G. (1986) *Coping with threatened identities*, London: Methuen.

Brent, J. (1997) 'Community without unity', in P. Hoggett (ed) *Contested communities: Experience, struggles, policies*, Bristol: The Policy Press.

Bronfenbrenner, U. (1977) 'Towards an experimental ecology of human development', *American Psychologist*, vol 3, pp 513-31.

Bryant, R. (1997) 'The road to nowhere: the Barton by-pass campaign', *Community Development Journal*, vol 32, no 1, pp 77-86.

Bryman, A. (1992) *Charisma and leadership in organisations*, London: Sage Publications.

Bullen, P. and Onyx, J. (1998) *Measuring social capital in five communities in New South Wales: an analysis*, CACOM Working Paper series No 41, Sydney: Centre for Australian Community Organisations and Management.

Bulmer, M. (1987) *The social basis of community care*, London: Unwin Hyman.

Bunch, C. (1990)' Making common cause: diversity and coalitions', in L. Albrecht and R. Brewer (eds) *Bridges of power: Women's multi-cultural alliances*, Philadelphia, PA: New Society.

Burgess, P., Hall, S., Mawson, J. and Pearce, G. (2001) *Devolved approaches to local governance: Policy and practice in neighbourhood management*, York: Joseph Rowntree Foundation.

Burgoon, J.K. (1981) 'Non-verbal communication', in M. Ruffner and M. Burgoon (eds) *Interpersonal communication*, New York, NY: Holt, Rinehart and Winston.

Burns, D. (1992) *Poll tax rebellion*, Edinburgh: AK Press.

Burns, D. (1997) *Decentralisation: Towards a new system of accountability in local government*, Edinburgh: COSLA.

Burns, D. and Taylor, M. (1998) *Mutual aid and self-help: Coping strategies for excluded communities*, Bristol/York: The Policy Press/Joseph Rowntree Foundation.

Burns, D. and Taylor, M. (2000) *Auditing community participation: An assessment handbook*, Bristol/York: The Policy Press/Joseph Rowntree Foundation.

Burns, D., Hambleton, R. and Hoggett, P. (1994) *The politics of decentralisation*, Basingstoke: Macmillan.

Burns, D., Williams, C.C. and Windebank, J. (2004) *Community self help*, Basingstoke: Palgrave.

Burns, D., Forrest, R., Flint, J. and Kearns, A. (2001) *Empowering communities: The impact of registered social landlords on social capital*, Research Report 94, Edinburgh: Scottish Homes.

Burns, T. and Stalker, G.M. (1961) *The management of innovation*, London: Tavistock.

Burt, R. (1997) 'A note on social capital and network content', *Social Networks*, vol 19, pp 355-74.

Butcher, H. (1993) 'Introduction: some examples and definitions', in H. Butcher, A. Glen, P. Henderson and J. Smith (eds) *Community and public policy*, London: Pluto Press.

Butt, J. (2001) 'Partnership and power: the role of black and minority ethnic voluntary organisations in challenging racism', in S. Balloch and M. Taylor (eds) *Partnership working: Policy and practice*, Bristol: The Policy Press.

Byrne, D. (1998) *Complexity theory and the social sciences*, London: Routledge.

Byrnoe, I. and Oliver, M. (1991) *Equal rights for disabled people*, London: Public Policy Research Unit.

Cammett, J.M. (1967) *Antonio Gramsci and the origins of Italian communism*, Stanford, CA: Stanford University Press.

Campbell, B. (1984) *Wigan Pier re-visited*, London: Virago.

Campbell, B. (1993) *Goliath*, London: Virago.

Cantle, T. (2001) *Community cohesion: A report of the independent review team*, London: Home Office.

Capra, F. (1996) *The web of life: A new synthesis of mind and matter*, London: HarperCollins.

Castells, M. (1983) *The city and the grassroots*, Berkeley, CA: University of California Press.

Castells, M. (1996) *The rise of the network society: The information age: Economy, society and culture*, Oxford: Blackwell.

Castells, M. (1997) *The power of identity: The information age: Economy, society and culture*, Oxford: Blackwell.

CDF (Community Development Foundation) (1996) *Regeneration and the community: Guidelines to the community involvement aspect of the SRB Challenge Fund*, London: CDF.

Chanan, G. (1991) *Taken for granted*, London: CDF.

Chanan, G. (1992) *Out of the shadows*, Dublin: European Foundation for the Improvement of Living and Working Conditions.

Chanan, G. (1997) *Active citizenship: Getting to the roots*, Dublin: European Foundation for the Improvement of Living and Working Conditions.

Chanan, G. (1999) *Local community involvement: A handbook for good practice*, Dublin: European Foundation for the Improvement of Living and Working Conditions.

Chanan, G. (2003) *Searching for solid foundations: Community involvement and urban policy*, London: ODPM.

Chanan, G. and Vos, K. (1990) *Social change and local action: Coping with disadvantage in urban areas*, Dublin: European Foundation for the Improvement of Living and Working Conditions.

Chanan, G., Garrett, C. and West, A. (2000) *The new community strategies*, London: CDF.

Chaney, P. (2000) 'Social capital and community development', *Journal of Community Work and Development*, vol 6, pp 51-8.

Chayko, M. (2002) *Connecting: How we form social bonds and communities in the internet age*, Albany, NY: State University of New York Press.

Cheater, A. (1999) 'Power in the post-modern era', in A. Cheater (ed) *The anthropology of power: Empowerment and disempowerment in changing structures*, London: Routledge.

Christian, M. (1998) 'Empowerment and Black communities in the UK', *Community Development Journal*, vol 33, no 1, pp 18-31.

Cilliers, P. (1998) *Complexity and post-modernism*, London: Routledge.

Clarke, R. (ed) (1990) *Enterprising neighbours: The development of the Community Association Movement in Britain*, London: National Federation of Community Organisations.

Clarke, T. (1963) *Working with communities*, London: National Council of Social Services.

Clegg, S. (1989) *Frameworks of power*, London: Sage Publications.

Clegg, S. (1990) *Modern organisations: Organisation studies in the post-modern world*, London: Sage Publications.

Clegg, S. (1994) 'Weber and Foucault: social theory for the study of organisations', *Organisation*, vol 1, no 1, pp 149-78.

Clegg, S. and Hardy, C. (1996) 'Conclusion: representations', in S. Clegg, C. Hardy and W.R. Nord (eds) *Handbook of organisation studies*, London: Sage Publications.

Clutterbuck, D. (1994) *The power of empowerment*, London: Kogan Page.

Coates, J. (1986) *Women, men and language*, London: Longman.

Cohen, A. (ed) (1974) *Urban ethnicity*, London: Tavistock.

Cohen, A. (1985) *The symbolic construction of community*, London: Routledge.

Cohen, A. (ed) (1986) *Symbolising boundaries: Identity and diversity in British cultures*, Manchester: Manchester University Press.

Cohen, J. and Stewart, I. (1994) *The collapse of chaos: Discovering simplicity in a complex world*, New York, NY: Viking.

Cole, J. (1997) *About face*, Cambridge, MA: MIT Press.

Cole, K.C. (1984) *Sympathetic vibrations: Reflections on physics as a way of life*, New York, NY: Bantum Books.

Colebatch, H. and Lamour, P. (1993) *Market, bureaucracy and community*, London: Pluto Press.

Coleman, J. (1988) 'Social capital in the creation of human capital', *American Journal of Sociology*, vol 94, pp 95-120.

Coleman, J. (1990) *Foundations of social theory*, Cambridge, MA: Harvard University Press.

Community Development Project (1974) *Inter-project report*, London: Community Development Project Information Intelligence Unit.

Community Development Project (1977) *Gilding the ghetto: The state and the poverty experiment*, London: Community Development Project Information Intelligence Unit.

Cooke, I. and Shaw, M. (eds) (1996) *Radical community work: Perspectives from practice in Scotland*, Edinburgh: Moray House Institute of Education.

Cooper, D. (1998) 'Regard between strangers: diversity, equality and the reconstruction of public space', *Critical Social Policy*, vol 18, no 4, pp 465-92.

Cooper, R. and Burrell, G. (1988) 'Modernism, post-modernism and organisational analysis', *Organisation*, vol 9, pp 91-112.

Corrigan, P. and Leonard, P. (1978) 'Community work and politics', in P. Corrigan and P. Leonard (eds) *Social work practice under capitalism: A Marxist approach*, London: Macmillan.

Coulson, A. (1998) *Trust and contracts*, Bristol: The Policy Press.

Cowley, J. (1977) 'The politics of community organising', in J. Cowley (ed) *Community or class struggle?*, London: Stage One.

Craig, G. (1998) 'Community development in a global context', *Community Development Journal*, vol 33, pp 2-17.

Craig, G. and Mayo, M. (eds) (1995) *Community and empowerment: A reader in participation and development*, London: Zed Books.

Crow, G. and Allan, G. (1994) *Community life*, Hemel Hempstead: Harvester Wheatsheaf.

Crowther, J., Martin, I. and Shaw, M. (1999) *Popular education and social movements in Scotland today*, Leicester: NIACE.

CRU (Civil Renewal Unit) (2003) *Building civil renewal: A review of government support for community capacity building and proposals for change*, London: Home Office.

Curtis, R.L. and Zurcher, L.A. (1973) 'Stable resources of protest movements: the multi-organisational field', *Social Forces*, vol 52, pp 53-61.

Dahl, R.A. (1961) *Who governs? Democracy and power in an American city*, New Haven, CT: Yale University Press.

Davis, A. (1981) *Women, race and class*, New York, NY: Vintage.

Dawson, S. (1996) *Analysing organisations*, Basingstoke: Macmillan.

de Groot, A.D. (1965) *Thought and choice in chess*, The Hague: Mouton.

Dennett, D. (1991) *Consciousness explained*, London: Little Brown.

Dennis, N., Henriques, F. and Slaughter, C. (1969) *Coal is our life: An analysis of a Yorkshire mining community*, London: Tavistock.

Derricourt, N. and Dale, J. (1994) 'Mapping the community work minefield', in S. Jacobs and K. Popple (eds) *Community work in the 1990s*, Nottingham: Spokesman.

Digeser, P. (1992) 'The fourth face of power', *Journal of Politics*, vol 54, pp 977-1007.

Dominelli, L. (1990) *Women and community action*, Birmingham: Venture Press.

Dominelli, L. (1995) 'Women in the community: feminist principles and organising in community work', *Community Development Journal*, vol 30, pp 133-43.

Doucet, A. (2000) '"There's a huge gulf between me as a male carer and women': gender domestic responsibility and the community as an institutional arena', *Community, Work and Family*, vol 3, no 3, pp 163-84.

Douglass, F. (1857) 'No progress without struggle!', An address on West Indian Emancipation (4 August).

Dreyfus, H.L. and Dreyfus, S.E. (1986) *Mind over machine: The power of intuition and expertise in the era of the computer*, New York, NY: The Free Press.

du Toit, A.-M. (1998) 'Building cultural synergy and peace in South Africa', *Community Development Journal*, vol 33, no 2, pp 80-90.

Duck, S. (1991) *Friends for life: The psychology of personal relationships*, Hemel Hempstead: Harvester Wheatsheaf.

Duck, S. (1992) *Human relationships*, London: Sage Publications.

Dunbar, R. (1996) *Grooming, gossip and the evolution of language*, London: Faber and Faber.

Durkheim, E. (1893) *The division of labour in society*, London: Macmillan.

Easton, G. (1996) 'Only connect: networks and organisations', *Organization*, vol 3, pp 291-310.

Egan, G. (1986) *The skilled helper*, Monterey, CA: Brooks Cole.

Eibl-Eibesfeldt, I. (1989) *Human ethology*, New York, NY: Aldine de Gruyter.

Elias, N. and Scotson, J. (1965) *The established and the outsiders*, London: Frank Cass.

Elsdon, K. (1998) *Studying local organisations: Purpose, methods and findings*, London: CDF.

Elworthy, S. (1996) *Power and sex: A book about women*, Shaftesbury: Element Books.

Emery, F.E. and Trist, E.L. (1965) 'The causal texture of organisational environments', *Human Relations*, vol 18, pp 21-31.

Emler, N. (1994) 'Gossip, reputation and social adaptation', in R.F. Goodman and A. Ben-Ze'ev (eds) *Good gossip*, Kansas, TX: University Press of Kansas.

Eraut, M. (1994) *Developing professional knowledge and competence*, London: Falmer.

Erikson, K. (1976) *Everything in its path*, New York, NY: Simon and Shuster.

Erikson, K. (1979) *In the wake of the flood*, London: Allen and Unwin.

Erskine, A. and Breitenbach, E. (1994) *Evaluation in community development*, Policy for Practice papers, no 1, Glasgow: Scottish Community Development Centre.

Estrella, M. and Gaventa, J. (1998) *Who counts reality? Participatory monitoring and evaluation: A literature review*, Brighton: Institute of Development Studies, University of Sussex

Etzioni, A. (1993) *The spirit of community*, New York, NY: Crown Books

Eve, R. (1997) 'Afterword: so where are we now? A final word', in R. Eve (ed) *Chaos, complexity and sociology*, Thousand Oaks, CA: Sage Publications.

FCWTGs (Federation of Community Work Training Groups) (2002) *The national occupational standards in community development*, Sheffield: FCWTGs.

Fearon, K. (1999) *Women's work: The study of the Northern Ireland Women's Coalition*, Belfast: Blackstaff Press.

Fehr, B. (1996) *Friendship processes*, London: Sage Publications.

Ferguson, K. (1984) *The feminist case against bureaucracy*, Philadelphia, PA: Temple University Press.

Ferree, M.M. (1992) 'The political context of rationality: rational choice theory and resource mobilisation', in A.D. Morris and C. McClurg Mueller (eds) *Frontiers in social movement theory*, New Haven, CT: Yale University Press.

Field, J. (2003) *Social capital*, London: Routledge.

Filkin, E. and Naish, M. (1982) 'Whose side are we on? The damage done by neutralism', in G. Craig, N. Derricourt and M. Loney (eds) *Community work and the state*, London: Routledge and Kegan Paul.

Fine, B. (2000) *Social capital versus social theory: Political economy and social science at the turn of the millennium*, London: Routledge.

Fineman, S. (1993) 'Organisations as emotional arenas', in S. Fineman (ed) *Emotions in organisations*, London: Sage Publications.

Fineman, S. and Gabriel, Y. (1996) *Experiencing organisations*, London: Sage Publications.

Finnegan, R. (1989) *The hidden musicians*, Cambridge: Cambridge University Press.

Firth, H. and Rapley, M. (1990) *From acquaintance to friendship: Issues for people with learning disabilities*, Kidderminster: BIMH Publications.

Fischer, C. (1982) *To dwell amongst friends: Personal networks in town and city*, Chicago, IL: University of Chicago Press.

Flecknoe, C. and McLellan, N. (1994) *The what, how and why of neighbourhood community development* (3rd edn), London: Community Matters.

Fleetwood, M. and Lambert, J. (1982) 'Bringing socialism home: theory and practice for a radical community action', in G. Craig, N. Derricourt and M. Loney (eds) *Community work and the state*, London: Routledge and Kegan Paul.

Flora, C. (1997) 'Building social capital: the importance of entrepreneurial social infrastructure', *Rural Development News*, vol 21, no 2, pp 1-3.

Flynn, M. (1989) 'The social environment', in A. Brechin and J. Walmsley (eds) *Making connections: Reflecting on the lives and experiences of people with learning difficulties*, London: Hodder and Stoughton.

Foley, M. and Edwards, B. (1999) 'Is it time to dis-invest in social capital?', *Journal of Public Policy*, vol 19 no 2, pp 141-73.

Forrest, R. and Kearns, A. (1999) *Joined up places? Social cohesion and neighbourhood regeneration*, York: Joseph Rowntree Foundation.

Forrest, R. and Kearns, A. (2001) *Social cohesion, social capital and neighbourhood change*, Bristol/York: The Policy Press/Joseph Rowntree Foundation.

Forster, E.M. (1910) *Howards End*, London: Edward Arnold.

Foucault, M. (1977) *Discipline and punishment*, Harmondsworth: Penguin.

Foucault, M. (1980) *Power/knowledge*, New York, NY: Pantheon.

Frances, J., Levacic, R., Mitchell, J. and Thompson, G. (1991) 'Introduction', in G. Thompson, J. Frances, R. Levacic and J. Mitchell (eds) *Markets, hierarchies and networks: The co-ordination of social life*, London: Sage Publications.

Francis, D., Henderson, P. and Thomas, D. (1984) *A survey of community workers in the United Kingdom*, London: NISW.

Frankenberg, R. (1966) *Communities in Britain: Social life in town and country*, Harmondsworth: Penguin.

Freeman, J. (1973) *The tyranny of structurelessness*, New York, NY: Falling Wall Press.

Freeman, L. (2000) 'Visualising social networks', *Journal of Social Structure*, vol 1, no 1, accessed at www.cmu.edu/joss/index1.html

Freeman, L., Webster, C. and Kirke, D. (1998) 'Exploring social structure using dynamic three dimensional color images', *Social Networks*, vol 20, pp 109-18.

Freire, P. (1972) *Pedagogy of the oppressed*, Harmondsworth: Penguin.

Fukuyama, F. (1996) *Trust: The social virtues and the creation of prosperity*, London: Hamilton.

Furbey, R., Else, P., Farnell, R., Lawless, P., Lund, S. and Wishart, B. (1997) 'Breaking with tradition? The Church of England and community organising', *Community Development Journal*, vol 32, no 2, pp 141-50.

Gabarino, J. (1983) 'Social support networks for the helping professions', in J. Whittaker and J. Gabarino (eds) *Social support networks: Informal helping in the human services*, Hawthorne, NY: Aldine DeGruyter.

Gaffney, M. (1996) 'Community development and partnership in practice', in B. Harbor, P. Morris and I. McCormack (eds) *Learning to disagree*, London/Dublin: Impact/Unison.

Gambetta, D. (ed) (1988) *Trust: Making and breaking co-operative relations*, Oxford: Basil Blackwell.

Gamble, C. (1999) *The paleolithic societies of Europe*, Cambridge: Cambridge University Press.

Gann, N. (1996) *Managing change in voluntary organisations: A guide to practice*, Buckingham: Open University Press.

Gans, H.F. (1962) *The urban villagers: Group and class in the life of Italian Americans*, New York, NY: Free Press.

Garrett, S. (1989) 'Friendship and the social order', in R. Porter and S. Tomaselli (eds) *The dialectics of friendship*, London: Routledge.

Gatehouse, M. (1982) 'A community building as a focus for neighbourhood work', in P. Henderson, A. Wright and K. Wyncoll (eds) *Successes and struggles on council estates: Tenants' action and community work*, Newcastle: Association of Community Workers.

Geddes, M. (1998) *Local partnership: A successful strategy for social cohesion*, Dublin: European Foundation for the Improvement of Living and Working Conditions.

Gilchrist, A. (1992a) 'Grey matters: struggles for new thinking and new respect', *Community Development Journal*, vol 27, pp 175-81.

Gilchrist, A. (1992b) 'The revolution of everyday life revisited: towards an anti-discriminatory praxis for community development work', *Social Action*, vol 1, pp 22-8.

Gilchrist, A. (1994) *Report and evaluation of the Bristol Festival Against Racism*, Bristol: Avon Race Equality Unit.

Gilchrist, A. (1995) *Community development and networking*, London: CDF.

Gilchrist, A. (1998a) '"A more excellent way": developing coalitions and consensus through informal networking', *Community Development Journal*, vol 33, no 2, pp 100-8.

Gilchrist, A. (1998b) 'Connectors and catalysts', *SCCD News*, no 18, pp 18-20.

Gilchrist, A. (1999) 'Serendipity and the snowflakes', *SCCD News*, no 19, pp 7-10.

Gilchrist, A. (2000) 'The well-connected community: networking to the "edge of chaos"', *Community Development Journal*, vol 35, pp 264-75.

Gilchrist, A. (2001) 'Strength through diversity: a networking approach to community development', unpublished PhD thesis, University of Bristol.

Gilchrist, A. (2003a) 'Linking partnerships and networks', in S. Banks, H. Butcher, P. Henderson and J. Robertson (eds) *Managing community practice*, Bristol: The Policy Press.

Gilchrist, A. (2003b) 'Community development and networking for health', in J. Orme, M. Grey, T. Harrison, J. Powell and P. Taylor (eds) *Public health for the 21st century: Policy, participation and practice*, Basingstoke: Open University Press/ McGraw Hill Education.

Gilchrist, A. (2003c) *Community cohesion: a community development approach*, ACW Talking Point No 204, Newcastle upon Tyne: Association of Community Workers.

Gilchrist, A. and Taylor, M. (1997) 'Community networking: developing strength through diversity', in P. Hoggett (ed) *Contested communities: Experiences, struggles, policies*, Bristol: The Policy Press.

Gilligan, C. (1982) *In a different voice: Psychological theory and women's development*, Cambridge, MA: Harvard University Press.

Gilroy, P. (1982) 'Steppin' out of Babylon: race, class and autonomy', in Centre for Cultural Studies (ed) *The empire strikes back: Race and racism in 70s Britain*, London: Hutchinson.

Gittell, R. and Vidal, A. (1998) *Community organising: Building social capital as a development strategy*, Thousand Oaks, CA: Sage Publications.

Gladwell, M. (2000) *The tipping point: How little things can make a big difference*, London: Little Brown.

Gleick, J. (1987) *Chaos: Making a new science*, New York, NY: Viking.

Glen. A., Henderson, P., Humm, J., Meszaros, H. with Gaffney, M. (2004) *A survey of community development workers in the UK*, London: CDF/SCCD.

Glenn, A. and Pearce, M. (1998) *Paid community work practice: An analysis of advertised posts*, Ilkley: Department of Applied and Community Studies, Bradford and Ilkley Community College.

Gluckman, M. (ed) (1952) *Order and rebellion in tribal Africa*, London: Cohen and West.

Goetschius, G.W. (1969) *Working with community groups*, London: Routledge and Kegan Paul.

Goffman, E. (1959) *The presentation of self in everyday life*, New York, NY: Doubleday.

Gordon, G. (1999) *The internet: //a philosophical inquiry*, London: Routledge.

Goss, S. and Kent, C. (1995) *Health and housing: Working together? A review of the extent of inter-agency working*, Bristol/York: The Policy Press/Joseph Rowntree Foundation.

Gottlieb, B.H. (1981) 'Social networks and social support in community mental health', in B.H. Gottlieb (ed) *Social networks and social support*, Beverly Hills, CA: Sage Publications.

Gouldner, A. (1960) 'The norm of reciprocity: a preliminary statement', *American Sociological Review*, vol 25, pp 161-79.

Gramsci, A. (1971) *Selections from the prison notebooks*, London: Lawrence and Wishart.

Granovetter, M. (1973) 'The strength of weak ties', *American Journal of Sociology*, vol 78, pp 1360-80.

Granovetter, M. (1974) *Getting a job; A study of contacts and careers*, Cambridge, MA: Harvard University Press.

Granovetter, M. (1978) 'Threshold models of collective behaviour', *American Journal of Sociology*, vol 78, pp 1420-43.

Granovetter, M. (1985) 'Economic action and social structure: the problem of embeddedness', *American Journal of Sociology*, vol 9, pp 481-510.

Green, G., Grimsley, M., Suokas, A., Jowitt, T. and Linacre, R. (2000) *Social capital, health and economy in the South Yorkshire coalfields*, Sheffield: Sheffield Hallam University.

Griffiths, H. (1981) 'Community work in the 80s: paid and voluntary action', in G. Poulton (ed) *Community work issues and practice in the 80s*, Southampton: Southern Council for Community Work Training.

Gutch, R. (1992) *Contracting out: lessons from the US*, London: NCVO.

Hall, E.T. (1966) *The hidden dimension*, New York, NY: Double Day.

Hall, J.A. (1984) *Non-verbal sex differences: Communication, accuracy and expressive styles*, Baltimore, MD: Johns Hopkins University Press.

Hall, P. (2000) 'Social capital in Britain', *British Journal of Politics*, vol 29, pp 417-61.

Hall, S. (1990) 'Cultural identity and diaspora', in J. Rutherford (ed) *Identity: Community, culture, difference*, London: Lawrence and Wishart.

Hall, S. and Jefferson, T. (eds) (1975) *Resistance through rituals: Youth subcultures in post-war Britain*, Birmingham: Centre for Contemporary Cultural Studies.

Halpern, D. (2001) 'Moral values, social trust and inequality – can values explain crime?', *British Journal of Criminology*, vol 41, pp 236-51.

Halpern, D. (2004: forthcoming) *Social capital*, Cambridge: Polity Press.

Hambleton, R., Essex, S., Mills, L. and Razzaque, K. (1995) *The collaborative council: A study of multi-agency work in practice*, York: Joseph Rowntree Foundation.

Hammond, K.R. (1980) *Human judgement and decision making*, New York, NY: Hemisphere.

Hampton, K. (2003) 'Grieving for a lost network: collective action in a wired suburb', *The Information Society*, vol 19, no 5, pp 1-13.

Hampton, K. and Wellman, B. (2002) 'Neighbouring in Netville: how the internet supports community and social capital in a wired suburb', *City and Community*, vol 2, no 4, pp 277-311.

Hampton, W. (1970) *Democracy and community: A study of politics in Sheffield*, Oxford: Oxford University Press.

Handy, C. (1988) *Understanding voluntary organisations*, Harmondsworth: Penguin.

Harbor, B., Morris, P. and McCormack, I. (eds) (1996) *Learning to disagree*, London/Dublin: UNISON/IMPACT.

Hardin, R. (1982) *Collective action*, Baltimore, MD: Johns Hopkins University Press.

Harifan, L.J. (1916) 'The rural school community centre,' *Annals of the American Academy of Political and Social Science*, vol 67, pp 130-8.

Harris, K. (2003) 'Keep your distance: remote communication, face-to-face and the nature of community', *The Journal of Community Work and Development*, vol 1, no 4, pp 5-28.

Harrison, L., Hoggett, P. and Jeffers, S. (1995) 'Race, ethnicity and community development', *Community Development Journal*, vol 30, pp 144-57.

Hastings, A., McArthur, A. and McGregor, A. (1996) *Less than equal: Community organisations and estate regeneration partnerships*, Bristol/York: The Policy Press/Joseph Rowntree Foundation.

Hastings, C. (1993) *The new organisation: Growing the culture of organizational networking*, Maidenhead: McGraw-Hill.

Heald, T. (1983) *Networks: Who we know and how we use them*, London: Hodder and Stoughton.

Hebb, D.O. (1949) *The organisation of behaviour*, New York, NY: John Wiley and Sons.

Hebdige, D. (1987) *Cut'n'mix: Culture, identity and Caribbean music*, London: Routledge.

Helgesen, S. (1990) *The female advantage: Women's ways of leadership*, New York, NY: Doubleday.

Henderson, P. (1997) *Social inclusion and citizenship in Europe: The contribution of community development*, The Hague: CEBSD.

Henderson, P. (2000) 'An historical perspective on community development in the UK - power, politics and radical action', in P. Ashton and A Hobbs (eds) *Communities developing for health*, Liverpool: Health for All.

Henderson, P. and Salmon, H. (1998) *Signposts to local democracy: Local governance, communitarianism and community development*, London: CDF.

Henderson, P. and Thomas, D.N. (1980) *Skills in neighbourhood work* (1st edn), London: Allen and Unwin.

Henderson, P. and Thomas, D.N. (1987) *Skills in neighbourhood work* (2nd edn), London: Allen and Unwin.

Henderson, P. and Thomas, D.N. (2002) *Skills in neighbourhood work* (3rd edn), London: Routledge.

Henning, C. and Leiberg, M. (1996) 'Strong ties or weak ties? Neighbourhood networks in a new perspective', *Scandinavian Housing and Planning Research*, vol 13, no 1, pp 3-26.

Heraud, B. (1975) 'The new towns: a philosophy of community', in P. Leonard (ed) *The sociology of community action*, Keele: Sociological Review.

Heron, J. (1996) *Co-operative inquiry: Research into the human condition*, London: Sage Publications.

Hillery, G. (1955) 'Definitions of community: areas of agreement', *Rural Sociology*, vol 20, pp 111-23.

Hindess, B. (1996) *Discourse of power: From Hobbes to Foucault*, Oxford: Blackwell.

Hirschmann, A. (1984) *Getting ahead collectively: Grassroots experience in Latin America*, New York, NY: Pergamon Press.

Hochschild, A.R. (1993) 'Preface', in S. Fineman (ed) *Emotions in organisations*, London: Sage Publications.

Hoggett, P. (ed) (1997) *Contested communities: Experiences, struggles, policies*, Bristol: The Policy Press.

Hoggett, P. and Miller, C. (2000) 'Working with emotions in community organisations', *Community Development Journal*, vol 35, no 4, pp 352-64.

Homans, G.C. (1950) *The human group*, London: Routledge & Kegan Paul.

Homer, C. (1995) 'Community development work – responding to community disaster', *Talking Points*, No 163, Newcastle-upon-Tyne: ACW.

Hope, A. and Timmell, S. (1984) *Training for transformation: A handbook for community workers*, Gweru: Mambo Press.

Hopkins, W.E. (1997) *Ethical dimensions of diversity*, Thousand Oaks, CA: Sage Publications.

Hopton, J. (1997) 'Anti-discriminatory practice and anti-oppressive practice', *Critical Social Policy*, vol 52, no 17, pp 47-61.

Hornby, S. (1993) *Collaborative care*, Oxford: Blackwell.

Hosking, D.-M. and Morley, I.E. (1991) *A social psychology of organising: People, processes and contexts*, London: Harvester Wheatsheaf.

House, J.S. and Landis, K.R. (1988) 'Social relationships and health', *Science*, vol 241, pp 540-5.

Humphries, B. and Martin, M. (2000) 'Unsettling the learning community: from "dialogue" to "difference"', *Community, Work and Family*, vol 3, no 3, pp 279-95.

Hunter, F. (1953) *Community power structure*, Chapel Hill, NC: University of North Carolina Press.

Hunter, A. and Staggenborg, S. (1988) 'Local communities and organised action', in C. Milofsky (ed) *Community organisations: Studies in resource mobilisation and exchange*, New York, NY: Oxford University Press.

Husteddes, R. and King, B. (2002) 'Rituals: emotions, community faith in soul and the messiness of life', *Community Development Journal*, vol 37, pp 338-48.

Hutton, W. (1995) *The state we're in*, London: Vintage.

Ife, J. (1995) *Community development: Creating community alternatives and practice*, Melbourne, Australia, Longman House.

Ikkink, K.K. and van Tilburg, T. (1998) 'Do older adults' network members continue to provide instrumental support in unbalanced relationships?', *Journal of Social and Personal Relationships*, vol 15, no 1, pp 59-75.

Ingamells, A. (1996) 'Constructing frameworks from practice', in J. Fook (ed) *The reflective researcher*, St Leonards, Australia: Allen and Unwin.

Inter-departmental Working Group on Resourcing Community Capacity Building (2001) *Funding community groups: A consultation document*, London: Active Community Unit, Home Office.

Jacobs, B.D. (1992) *Fractured cities: Capitalism, community and empowerment in Britain and America*, London and New York, NY: Routledge.

Jacobs, J. (1961) *The death and life of great American cities*, London: Cape.

Jacobs, M. (1995) *Sustainability and socialism*, London: SERA.

Jantsch, E. (1980) *The self-organising universe*, Oxford: Pergamon Press.

Jaworski, J. (1996) *Synchronicity: The inner path of leadership*, San Francisco, CA: Berrett-Köhler.

Jeffers, S., Hoggett, P. and Harrison, L. (1996) 'Race, ethnicity and community in three localities', *New Community*, vol 22, no 1, pp 111-26.

Jelfs, M. (1982) *Manual for action: Techniques to enable groups engaged in action for change to increase their effectiveness*, London: Action Resources Group.

Jenkins, R. (1996) *Social identity*, London: Routledge.

Jessop, B. (1997) 'The governance of complexity and the complexity of governance: preliminary remarks on some problems and limits of economic guidance', in A. Amin and J. Hausner (eds) *Beyond market and hierarchy: Interactive governance and social complexity*, Cheltenham: Edward Elgar Publishing Ltd.

Johnson, C. (1998) 'Afghanistan: NGOs and women in the front line', *Community Development Journal*, vol 33, no 2, pp 117-23.

Johnston, H., Laraña, E. and Gusfield, J. (1994) 'Identities, grievances and new social movements', in E. Laraña, H. Johnston and J. Gusfield (eds) *New social movements*, Philadelphia, PA: Temple University Press.

Jones, S.G. (1995) *CyberSociety: Computer-mediated communication and community*, London: Sage Publications.

Kadushin, C. (1982) 'Social density and mental health', in P. Marsden and N. Lin (eds) *Social structure and network analysis*, Beverly Hills, CA: Sage Publications.

Kanter, R. (1983) *The changemasters*, New York, NY: Simon and Schuster.

Kapferer, B. (1969) 'Norms and the manipulation of relationships in a work setting', in J.C. Mitchell (ed) *Social networks in urban situations*, Manchester: Manchester University Press.

Katz, D. and Kahn, R.L. (1966) *The social psychology of organisations*, New York, NY: John Wiley.

Kauffman, S. (1993) *The origins of order: Self-organisation and selection in evolution*, Oxford: Oxford University Press.

Kauffman, S. (1995) *At home in the universe: The search for the laws of complexity*, London: Penguin.

Kauffman, S. (2001) *Investigations*, Oxford: Oxford University Press.

Kawachi, I. (1996) 'A prospective study of social networks in relation to total mortality and cardiovascular disease in the USA', *Journal of Epidemiology and Community Health*, vol 50, pp 245-91.

Kay, A. (1974) 'Planning, participation and planners', in M. Mayo and D. Jones (eds) *Community work one*, London: Routledge and Kegan Paul.

Kelly, C. and Breinlinger, S. (1996) *The social psychology of collective action: Identity, justice and gender*, London: Taylor and Francis.

Kickert, W.J.M., Klijn, E.-K. and Koppenjan, J.F.M. (1997) *Managing complex networks: Strategies for the public sector*, London: Sage Publications.

King, M.L. (1967) *Chaos or community? Where do we go from here?*, London: Hodder and Stoughton.

Kirkwood, G. and Kirkwood, C. (1989) *Living adult education: Freire in Scotland*, Milton Keynes: Open University Press.

Klandermans, B. (1997) *The social psychology of protest*, Oxford: Blackwell.

Klein, J. (1973) *Training for the new helping professions*, London: Goldsmiths College.

Knoke, D. (1990a) *Organising for collective action: The political economies of association*, New York, NY: Aldine de Gruyter.

Knoke, D. (1990b) *Political networks: The structural perspective*, Cambridge: Cambridge University Press.

Knoke, D. and Kulinski, J.H. (1982) *Network analysis*, Beverley Hills, CA: Sage Publications.

Kolb, D. (1992) 'Women's work: peacemaking in organisations', in D. Kolb and J.M. Bartunek (eds) *Hidden conflict in organisations: Uncovering behind the scenes disputes*, Newbury Park, CA: Sage Publications.

Krackhardt, D. (1994) 'A picture's worth a thousand words', *Connections*, vol 16, pp 37-47.

Kreiner, K. and Schutz, M. (1990) *Crossing the institutional divide: Networking in bio-technology*, Copenhagen: Eureka Management Research Initiative.

Krishnamurthy, A., Prime, D. and Zimmeck, M. (2001) *Voluntary and community activities: Findings from the British Crime Survey 2000*, London: ACU research team, Home Office.

Kumar, S. (1997) *Accountability in the contract state*, York: Joseph Rowntree Foundation.

Kuzwe, C.N. (1998) 'The role of NGOs in democratisation and education in peacetime Rwanda', *Community Development Journal*, vol 33, no 2, pp 174-7.

Laguerre, M.S. (1994) *The informal city*, Basingstoke: Macmillan.

Landry, C. (1995) *The creative city: A toolkit for urban innovators*, London: Earthscan.

Landry, C., Morley, D., Southwood, R. and Wright, P. (1985) *What a way to run a railroad: An analysis of radical failure*, London: Comedia.

Lappe, F.M. and DuBois, P. (1997) 'Building social capital without looking backward', *National Civic Review*, vol 86, no 2, pp 119-28.

Laslett, P. (1956) 'The face-to-face society', in P. Laslett (ed) *Philosophy, politics and society*, Oxford: Blackwell.

Laumann, E. and Pappi, F. (1976) *Networks of collective action: A perspective on community influence systems*, New York, NY: Academic Press.

Leat, D. (1975) 'Social theory and the historical construction of social work activity', in P. Leonard (ed) *The sociology of community action*, Keele: Sociological Review.

Leat, D. (1988) *Voluntary organisations and accountability*, London: NCVO.

Ledwith, M. (1997) *Participating in transformation: Towards a working model of community empowerment*, Birmingham: Venture Press.

Ledwith, M. and Asgill, P. (2000) 'Critical alliance: Black and white women working together for social justice', *Community Development Journal*, vol 35, no 3, pp 290-9.

Lee, N.H. (1969) *The search for an abortionist*, Chicago, IL: University of Chicago Press.

Lees, R. and Mayo, M. (1984) *Community action for change*, London: Routledge. and Kegan Paul.

Leissner, A. (1975) 'Models for community work and community and youth workers', *Social Work Today*, vol 5, no 22, pp 669-75.

Levinger, G. (1980) 'Towards the analysis of close relationships', *Journal of Experimental Psychology*, vol 16, pp 510-44.

Levitas, R. (1998) *The inclusive society? Social inclusion and New Labour*, Basingstoke: Macmillan.

Lewin, K. (1936) *Principles of topological psychology*, London: McGraw-Hill.

Lewin, R. (1993) *Complexity: Life on the edge of chaos*, London: Phoenix.

Ling Wong, J. (1998) 'Ethnic community environmental participation', in D. Warburton (ed) *Community and sustainable development: Participation in the future*, London: Earthscan.

Lingayah, S. (2001) *Prove it! Measuring impacts of renewal: Findings and recommendations*, London: New Economics Foundation.

Lipnack, J. and Stamps, J. (1994) *The age of the network: Organising principles for the 21st century*, New York, NY: Wiley.

Lloyd, L. and Gilchrist, A. (1994) 'Community caremongering: principles and paradoxes', *Care in Place*, vol 1, pp 133-44.

LGA (Local Government Association) (2002) *Guidance on community cohesion*, London: LGA.

LGMB (Local Government Management Board) (1998) *Networks and networking*, Luton: LGMB.

LEWRG (London Edinburgh Weekend Return Group) (1979) *In and against the state*, London: Pluto Press.

Loney, M. (1983) *Community against government*, London: Heinemann.

Lovelock, J. (1979) *Gaia*, Oxford: Oxford University Press.

Lowe, S. (1986) *Urban social movements: The city after Castells*, Basingstoke: Macmillan.

Lowndes, V. (2000) 'Women and social capital: a comment on Hall's "social capital in Britain"', *British Journal of Politics*, vol 30, pp 533-40.

Lukes, S. (1974) *Power: A radical view*, Basingstoke: Macmillan.

Lyford, J. (2001) *Women's networking: A practical guide*, Produced and printed on behalf of the Women's Decision Making Network, Derby: Derby City Council.

McCabe, A., Lowdnes, V. and Skelcher, C. (1997) *Partnerships and networks*, York: Joseph Rowntree Foundation.

McClurg Mueller, C. (1994) 'Conflict networks and the origins of women's liberation', in E. Laraña, H. Johnston and J. Gusfield (eds) *New social movements*, Philadelphia, PA: Temple University Press.

McCrone, J. (1999) *Going inside: A tour round a single moment of consciousness*, London: Faber and Faber.

McCulloch, A. (1997) 'You've fucked up the estate and now you're carrying a brief case', in P. Hoggett (ed) *Contested communities: Experience, struggles, policies*, Bristol: The Policy Press.

MacGillivray, A. and Zadek, S. (1996) *Accounting for change: Indicators for sustainable development*, London: New Economics Foundation.

McPherson, J.M. (1983) 'The size of voluntary organisations', *Social Forces*, vol 61, pp 1044-64.

McPherson, J.M. (1988) 'A theory of voluntary organisation', in C. Milofsky (ed) *Community organisations: Studies in resource mobilisation and exchange*, New York, NY: Oxford University Press.

McWilliams, M. (1995) 'Struggling for peace and justice: reflections on women's activism in Northern Ireland', *Journal of Women's History*, vol 6/7, nos 4/1, p 13.

Maffesoli, M. (1996) *The time of the tribes: The decline of individualism in mass society*, London: Sage Publications.

Madanipour, A. (2003) *Public and private spaces of the city*, London: Routledge.

Marriott, P. (1997) *Forgotten resources? The role of community buildings in strengthening local communities*, York: Joseph Rowntree Foundation.

Marris, P. (1996) *The politics of uncertainty: Attachment in private and public life*, London: Routledge.

Marwell, G. and Oliver, P. (1993) *The critical mass in collective action: A micro-social theory*, Cambridge: Cambridge University Press.

Maslach, C. (1982) *Burnout: The cost of caring*, Englewood Cliffs, NJ: Prentice Hall.

Mason, D. (1996) *Leading and managing the expressive dimension: Harnessing the hidden power source of the voluntary sector*, San Francisco, CA: Jossey-Bass.

Massey, D. (1994) *Space, place and gender*, Cambridge: Polity Press.

Maturana, H.R. and Varela, F.J. (1987) *The tree of knowledge: The biological roots of human understanding*, Boston, MA: Shambhala.

May, N. (1997) *Challenging assumptions: Gender considerations in urban regeneration in the UK*, York: Joseph Rowntree Foundation.

Mayo, E. (1960) *The human problems of an industrial civilisation*, New York, NY: Viking Press.

Mayo, M. (1975) 'The history and early development of CDP', in R. Lees and M. Brake (eds) *Action research in community development*, London: Routledge and Kegan Paul.

Mayo, M. (ed) (1977) *Women in the community*, London: Routledge and Kegan Paul.

Mayo, M. (1979) 'Radical politics and community action', in M. Loney and M. Allen (eds) *The crisis in the inner-city*, London: Macmillan.

Mayo, M. (1994) *Communities and caring: The mixed economy of welfare*, Basingstoke: Macmillan.

Mayo, M. (1997a) *Imagining tomorrow: Adult education for transformation*, Leicester: NIACE.

Mayo, M. (1997b) 'Partnerships for regeneration and community development', *Critical Social Policy*, vol 17, no 52, pp 3-26.

Mayo, M. (2000) *Cultures, communities, identities: Cultural strategies for participation and empowerment*, London: Palgrave.

Mayo, M. and Taylor, M. (2001) 'Partnership and power in community regeneration', in S. Balloch and M. Taylor (eds) *Partnership working*, Bristol: The Policy Press.

Mayo, M. and Thompson, J. (eds) (1995) *Adult learning: Critical intelligence and social change*, Leicester: NIACE.

Mead, G.H. (1938) *The philosophy of the act* (edited by C.W. Morris), Chicago, IL: Chicago University Press.

Means, R., Brenton, M., Harrison, L. and Heywood, F. (1997) *Making partnerships work in community care: A guide for practitioners in housing, health and social services*, Bristol: The Policy Press.

Melucci, A. (1989) *Nomads of the present: Social movements and individual needs in contemporary society*, Philadelphia, PA: Temple University Press.

Melucci, A. (1996) *Challenging codes: Collective action in the information age*, Cambridge: Cambridge University Press.

Milgram, S. (1967) 'The small world problem', *Psychology Today*, vol 2, pp 60-7.

Miliband, R. (1969) *The state in capitalist society*, London: Weidenfeld and Nicholson.

Miller, C. and Ahmad, Y. (1997) 'Community development at the crossroads: a way forward', *Policy & Politics*, vol 25, no 3, pp 269-84.

Miller, C. and Bryant, R. (1990) 'Community work in the UK: reflections on the 1980s', *Community Development Journal*, vol 25, no 4, pp 316-25.

Miller, J. (1974) *Aberfan: A disaster and its aftermath*, London: Constable.

Miller, J.B. (1976) *Towards a new psychology of women*, Boston, MA: Beacon Press.

Miller, M. (1958) 'A comparative study of decision making in English and American cities', in C. Bell and C. Newby (eds) *Community studies*, London: George Allen and Unwin.

Milofsky, C. (1987) 'Neighbourhood-based organisations: a market analogy', in W.W. Powell (ed) *The non-profit sector: A research handbook*, New Haven, CT: Yale University Press.

Milofsky, C. (1988a) 'Introduction: networks, markets, cultures and contracts: understanding community organisations', in C. Milofsky (ed) *Community organisations: Studies in resource mobilisation and exchange*, New York, NY: Oxford University Press.

Milofsky, C. (1988b) 'Scarcity and community: a resource allocation theory of community and mass society organisations', in C. Milofsky (ed) *Community organisations: Studies in resource mobilisation and exchange*, New York, NY: Oxford University Press.

Milofsky, C. (1988c) 'Structure and process in community self-help organisations', in C. Milofsky (ed) *Community organisations: Studies in resource mobilisation and exchange*, New York, NY: Oxford University Press.

Milson, F. (1974) *Introduction to community work*, London: Routledge and Kegan Paul.

Mingers, J. (1995) *Self-producing systems: Implications and applications of autopoiesis*, New York, NY: Plenum Press.

Misztal, B. (2000) *Informality: Social theory and contemporary practice*, London: Routledge.

Mitchell, J.C. (ed) (1969) *Social networks in urban situations: Analyses of personal relationships in central African towns*, Manchester: Manchester University Press.

Mitchell, W.J. (1999) *E-topia: Urban life, Jim, but not as we know it*, Boston, MA: MIT Press.

Mithen, S. (1996) *The prehistory of the mind: A search for the origins of art, religion and science*, London: Thames and Hudson.

Modood, T. (1992) *Not easy being British: Colour, culture and citizenship*, Stoke on Trent: Runnymede Trust and Trentham Books.

Modood, T. (2003) 'New forms of Britishness: post-immigration ethnicity and hybridity in Britain', in R. Sackmann, B. Peters and T. Faust (eds) *Identity and integration: Migrants in Western Europe*, Aldershot: Ashgate.

Mondros, J. and Wilson, S. (1994) *Organising for power and empowerment*, New York, NY: Columbia University Press.

Moreno, J. (1934) *Who shall survive? A new approach to the problem of human inter-relations*, New York, NY: Beacon Press.

Morgan, G. (1986) *Images of organisation*, Newbury Park, CA: Sage Publications.

Morgan, G. (1989) *Creative organisation theory: A resource book*, London: Sage Publications.

Morris, A.D. (1992) 'Political consciousness and collective action', in A.D. Morris and C. McClurg Muller (eds) *Frontiers in social movement theory*, New Haven, CT: Yale University Press.

Morris, J. (1991) *Pride against prejudice*, London: Women's Press.

Morrisey, J. (2000) 'Indicators of citizen participation: lessons from learning teams in rural EZ/EC communities', *Community Development Journal*, vol 35, no 1, pp 59-74.

Moser, C. and Holland, J. (1997) *Urban poverty and violence in Jamaica*, Latin American and Caribbean Studies Series, Washington, DC: World Bank.

Mulgan, G. (1997) *Connexity: How to live in a connected world*, London: Chatto and Windus.

Mullender, A. and Ward, D. (1991) *Self-directed groupwork: Users taking action for empowerment*, London: Whiting and Birch.

Murdoch, J. and Day, G. (1995) 'Two narratives of community: from exclusion to the construction of diversity', Paper presented to Ideas of Community conference at University of the West of England, September.

Murdock, G.P. (1945) 'The common denominator of cultures', in R. Linton (ed) *The science of man in the world*, New York, NY: Columbia University Press.

Narroll, R. (1983) *The moral order*, Beverly Hills, CA: Sage Publications.

Narayan, D. and Pritchett, L. (1997) *Cents and sociability: Household income and social capital in rural Tanzania*, Social Development and Development Research Group, Policy Research Paper No 1796, Washington, DC: World Bank.

Nash, V. (ed) (2002) *Reclaiming community*, London: IPPR.

Nash V. and Christie, I. (2003) *Making sense of community*, London: IPPR.

Nelson, C., Dickinson, S., Beetham, M. and Batsleer, J. (2000) 'Border crossings/translations: resources of hope in community work with women in Greater Manchester', *Community, Work and Family*, vol 3, no 3, pp 349-62.

Newby, H. (1977) *The deferential worker: A study of farm workers in East Anglia*, London: Allen Lane.

Newcomb, T.M. (1961) *The acquaintance process*, New York, NY: Holt, Rinehart and Winston.

Newman, I. and Geddes, M. (2001) 'Developing local strategies for social inclusion', Paper presented to Local Authorities and Social Exclusion programme, Local Government Centre, Warwick University, March.

Nietzsche, F. (1878) 'Thus spoke Zarathutra', in *The portable Nietzsche* (edited and translated by W. Kaufmann, 1971), London: Chatto & Windus.

Nisbet, R.A. (1953) *The quest for community*, Oxford: Oxford University Press.

Nohria, N. and Eccles, R.G. (1992) 'Face-to-face: making network organisations work', in N. Nohria and R.G. Eccles (eds) *Networks and organisations: Structure, form and action*, Boston, MA: Harvard Business School.

Norman, A.J. (1993) 'Building multi-ethnic coalitions with public sector organisations: an expanded dialogue model', in E.-Y.Yu and E.T. Chang (eds) *Multi-ethnic coalition building*, Los Angeles, CA: Regnia Books.

NRU (Neighbourhood Renewal Unit) (2002) *Collaboration and co-ordination in area-based intiatives*, Research Summary No 1, London: ODPM.

NRU (2003) *Review of community participation: Report for public consultation*, London: ODPM.

Ohri, A. (1998) *The world in our neighbourhood*, London: Development Education Association.

Ohri, A. and Manning, B. (eds) (1982) *Community work and racism*, London: Association of Community Workers.

Oldenberg, R. (1991) *The great good place: Cafes, coffee shops, community centres, beauty parlours, general stores, bars, hangouts, and how they get you through the day*, New York, NY: Paragon House.

Oliver, M. (1996) *Understanding disability*, London: Macmillan.

Olson, M. (1965) *The logic of collective action: Public goods and the theory of groups*, Cambridge, MA: Harvard University Press.

O'Malley, J. (1977) *The politics of community action: A decade of struggle in Notting Hill*, Nottingham: Spokesman.

ONS (Office for National Statistics) (2001) *Social capital: A review of the literature*, London: Social Analysis and Reporting Division, ONS.

Ornisch, D. (1999) *Love and survival: The scientific basis for the healing power of intimacy*, London: Vermillion.

Ouchi, W.G. (1980) 'Markets, bureaucracies and clans', *Administrative Science Quarterly*, vol 25, pp 129-41.

Oyserman, D. and Packer, M.J. (1996) 'Social cognition and self-concept: a socially contextualised model of identity', in J.L. Nye and A.M. Brower (eds) *What's social about social cognition?*, Thousand Oaks, CA: Sage Publications.

Pahl, R. (2000) *On friendship*, Cambridge: Polity Press.

Parekh, B. (2000) *The future of multi-racial Britain*, London: Profile Books.

Parikh, J. (1999) *Managing relationships*, Oxford: Capstone.

Park, R. (ed) (1925) *The city*, Chicago, IL: University of Chicago Press.

Park, R. (1929) *Human communities: The city and human ecology*, Glencoe, IL: Free Press.

Parker, M. (1992) 'Post-modern organisations or post-modern organisation theory?', *Organisation*, vol 13, pp 1-17.

PAT9 (1999) Report of the Policy Action Team on Community Self-help, London: Social Exclusion Unit.

Paton, R. (1996) 'How are values handled in voluntary agencies?', in D. Billis and M. Harris (eds) *Voluntary agencies: Challenges of organisation and management*, Basingstoke: Macmillan.

Patterson, M. (1991) 'A functional approach to non-verbal exchange', in R.S. Feldman and B.W.A. Rime (eds) *Fundamentals of non-verbal behaviour*, Cambridge: Cambridge University Press.

Paxman, J. (1990) *Friends in high places: Who runs Britain?*, London: Joseph.

Payne, M. (1982) *Working in teams*, London: Macmillan.

Payne, M. (1993) *Linkages: Effective networking in social care*, London: Whiting and Birch.

Perlman, H.H. (1979) *Relationships: The heart of helping people*, Chicago, IL: University of Chicago Press.

Perrow, C. (1979) *Complex organisations: A critical essay*, Dallas: Scott Forseman.

Perrow, C. (1992) 'Small firm networks', in N. Nohria and R. Eccles (eds) *Networks and organisations*, Boston, MA: Harvard Business School Press.

Phillips, A. (1987) *Divided loyalties: The dilemmas of sex and class*, London: Virago.

Phillips, A. (1994) 'Pluralism, solidarity and change', in J. Weeks (ed) *The lesser evil and the greater good*, London: River Orams Press.

Pilisuk, M. and Parks, S.H. (1986) *The healing web: Social networks and human survival*, Hanover, MA: University Press of New England.

Pindar, S. (1994) 'Planning a network response to racial harassment', in C. Ritchie, A. Taket and J. Bryant (eds) *Community works*, Sheffield: Pavic Publishing.

PIU (Performance and Innovation Unit) (2002) *Social capital: A discussion paper*, London: Cabinet Office.

Plowden, B.H. (1967) *Children and their schools*, London: HMSO.

Popple, K. (1995) *Analysing community work*, Buckingham: Open University Press.

Portes, A. and Landolt, P. (1996) 'The downside of social capital', *The American Prospect*, vol 26, pp 18-21.

Powell, W. (1990) 'Neither market, nor hierarchy: network forms of organisation', *Research in Organisational Behaviour*, vol 12, pp 295-336.

Power, M. (1994) *The audit explosion*, London: Demos.

Pryce, K. (1979) *Endless pressure: A study of West Indian life styles in Bristol*, Harmondsworth: Penguin.

Purdue, D. (2001) 'Neighbourhood governance: leadership, trust and social capital', *Urban Studies*, vol 38, no 12, pp 2211-24.

Purdue, D., Razzaque, K., Hambleton, R. and Stewart, M. (2000) *Community leadership in urban regeneration*, Bristol/York: The Policy Press/Joseph Rowntree Foundation.

Putnam, R. (1993) 'The prosperous community', *The American Prospect*, vol 13, no 4, pp 11-18.

Putnam, R. (1995) 'Bowling alone: America's declining social capital', *Journal of Democracy*, vol 6, pp 65-78.

Putnam, R. (2000) *Bowling alone: The collapse and revival of American community*, London: Simon and Shuster.

Putnam, R. (2001) 'Social capital: measurement and consequences', *Isuma – Canadian Journal of Policy Research*, vol 2, no 1, pp 41-52.

Qaiyoom, R. (1992) *From crisis to consensus: A strategic approach for local government and the Black voluntary sector*, London: SIA.

Rahman, M.A. (1993) *People's self-development: Perspectives on participatory action research: A journey through experience*, London: Zed Books.

Rattansi, A. (2002) *Whose British? Prospect and the new assimilation: Cohesion, community and citizenship*, London: Runnymede Trust.

RCU (Regional Coordination Unit) (2003) *Building civil renewal*, London: Home Office.

Redcliffe-Maude, J. (1969) *Report of the Royal Commission on Local Government in England 1966-1969*, London: HMSO.

Rees, S. (1991) *Achieving power: Practice and policy in social welfare*, London: Allen and Unwin.

Reinold, P. (1974) *Creative living*, London: National Federation of Community Associations.

Rex, J. and Moore, R. (1967) *Race, community and conflict: A study of Sparkbrook*, London: Oxford University Press.

Rheingold, H. (1993) *The virtual community*, San Francisco, CA: Addison-Wesley.

Richardson, L. and Mumford, K. (2002) 'Community, neighbourhood and social infrastructure', in J. Hills and J. LeGrand (eds) *Understanding social exclusion*, Oxford: Oxford University Press.

Roschelle, A.R. (1997) *No more kin: Exploring race, class and gender in family networks*, London: Sage Publications.

Rose, S. (1998) *From brains to consciousness*, London: Allen Lane.

Ross, E. (1983) 'Survival networks: women's neighbourhood sharing in London before World War 1', *History Workshop*, vol 15, pp 4-27.

Rupp, L. and Taylor, V. (1987) *Survival in the doldrums: The American women's rights movement, 1945-1960s*, New York, NY: Oxford University Press.

Rutherford, J. (ed) (1990) *Identity: Community, culture, difference*, London: Lawrence and Wishart.

Sabel, C.F. (1989) 'Flexible specialisation and the re-emergence of regional economies', in P. Hirst and J. Zeitlin (eds) *Reversing industrial decline?*, Oxford: Berg.

Sampson, R., Raudensbusch, S. and Earls, F. (1997) 'Crime: a multi-level study of collective efficacy', *Science*, vol 277, pp 918-24.

Saranson, S.B. (1976) 'Community psychology: networks and Mr Everyman', *American Psychologist*, May, pp 317-28.

SCCD (Standing Conference for Community Development) (2001) *Strategic framework for community work*, Sheffield: SCCD.

SCCD (2003) *Resource pack to promote networking for community development*, Sheffield: SCCD.

Schattschneider, E.E. (1960) *The sovereign people*, New York, NY: Holt, Rinehart and Wilson.

Schneiderman, L. (1988) *The psychology of social change*, New York, NY: Human Sciences Press.

Schön, D. (1990) *The reflective practitioner: How professionals think in action*, Aldershot: Avebury.

Schuler, D. (1996) *New community networks: Wired for change*, San Francisco, CA: Addison-Wesley.

Scott, A. (1990) *Ideology and the new social movements*, London: Unwin Hyman.

Scott, J. (1991) *Social network analysis: A handbook*, London: Sage Publications.

Scott, J.C. (1990) *Domination and the arts of resistance*, London: Yale University Press.

Scott, S., Houston, D. and Sterling, R. (2002) *Working together, learning together: An evaluation of the national training programme for social inclusion partnerships*, Glasgow: Department of Urban Studies, University of Glasgow.

Scott, W.R. (1992) *Organisations: Rational, natural and open systems*, Englewood Cliffs, NJ: Prentice Hall.

Seebohm, F. (1968) *Report of the Committee on Local Authority and Allied Personal Social Services*, London: HMSO.

Seed, P. (1990) *Introducing network analysis in social work*, London: Jessica Kingsley.

Seron, C. and Ferris, K. (1995) 'Negotiating professionalism: the gendered social capital of flexible time', *Work and Occupations*, vol 22, pp 22-47.

Servian, R. (1996) *Theorising empowerment: Individual power and community care*, Bristol: The Policy Press.

SEU (Social Exclusion Unit) (2000) *National Strategy for Neighbourhood Renewal: A framework for consultation*, London: The Stationery Office.

SEU (2001) *Action plan for neighbourhood renewal*, London: The Stationery Office.

Seyfang, G. and Smith, K. (2002) *The time of our lives: Using timebanking for neighbourhood renewal and community capacity building*, London: New Economics Foundation.

Shaw, M. and Martin, I. (2000) 'Community work, citizenship and democracy: remaking the connections', *Community Development Journal*, vol 35, no 4, pp 401-13.

Shuftan, C. (1996) 'The community development dilemma: what is really empowering?', *Community Development Journal*, vol 31, no 3, pp 260-4.

Shuftan, C. (1999) 'Sustainable development beyond ethical pronouncements: the role of civil society and networking', *Community Development Journal*, vol 34, no 3, pp 232-9.

Shukra, K. (1995) 'From Black power to Black perspectives: the reconstruction of a Black political identity', *Youth and Policy*, vol 49, pp 5-17.

Sik, E. and Wellman, B. (1999) 'Network capital in capitalist, communist and post-communist countries', in B. Wellman (ed) *Networks in the global village*, Boulder, CO: Westview Press.

Simmel, G. (1955) *'Conflict' and 'the web of group-affiliations'*, New York, NY: Free Press.

Simmie, J. (ed) (1997) *Innovation, networks and learning regions*, London: Jessica Kingsley Publishers.

Sivanandan, A. (1990) 'All that melts into air is solid: the hokum of New Times', *Race and Class*, vol 31, no 3, pp 1-30.

Skeffington, A.M. (1969) *People and planning: Report of the Committee on Public Participation in Planning*, London: HMSO.

Skelcher, C., McCabe, A., Lowndes, V. and Nanton, P. 1996) *Community networks in urban regeneration*, Bristol/York: The Policy Press/Joseph Rowntree Foundation.

Skinner, S. and Wilson, M. (2002) *Assessing community strengths*, London: CDF.

Smith, G. (1996) 'Ties, nets and an elastic Bund: community in the postmodern city', *Community Development Journal*, vol 37, no 1, pp 167-77.

Smith, G. (1999) 'IT rams CD', *SCCD News*, No 21, Autumn, pp 9-16.

Smith, M. (1994) *Local education*, Buckingham: Open University Press.

Smyth, J. (2001) 'Social capital and community involvement', Unpublished paper for Urban Forum conference, 5-6 December.

Sondhi, R. (1997) 'The politics of equality or the politics of difference? Locating Black communities in Western society', *Community Development Journal*, vol 32, no 3, pp 223-32.

Specht, H. (1976) *The community development project: National and local strategies for improving the delivery of services*, NISW Social Work Paper No 2, London: NISW.

Squires, J. (1994) 'Ordering the city: public spaces and political participation', in J. Weeks (ed) *The lesser evil and the greater good*, London: River Orams Press.

Stacey, M. (1969) 'The myth of community studies', *British Journal of Sociology*, vol 20, no 2, pp 134-47.

Stack, C. (1974) *All our kin: strategies for survival in a Black community*, New York, NY: Harper and Row.

Stackman, R. W. and Pinder, C.C. (1999) 'Context and sex effects on personal work networks', *Journal of Social and Personal Relationships*, vol 16, no 1, pp 39-64.

Standards Council for Community Work Training and Qualifications (England) (2000) *Community work occupational standards*, Sheffield: Federation of Community Work Training Groups.

Stephenson, K. (1998) 'Of human bonding', *People Management*, 29 October, pp 54-8.

Stewart, M. (1998) 'Accountability in community contributions to sustainable development', in D. Warburton (ed) *Community and sustainable development: Participation in the future*, London: Earthscan.

Stewart, M. (2000) 'Community governance', in H. Barton (ed) *Sustainable communities: The potential for community neighbourhoods*, London: Earthscan.

Stewart, M. and Taylor, M. (1995) *Empowerment in estate regeneration*, Bristol: The Policy Press.

Stone, A.R. (1991) 'Will the real body please stand up: boundary stories about virtual culture', in M. Benedikt (ed) *Cyberspace: First steps*, Cambridge, MA: MIT Press.

Sullivan, A. (1998) *Love undetectable*, London: Chatto and Windus.

Suttles, G. (1972) *The social construction of communities*, Chicago, IL: University of Chicago Press.

Symons, B. (1981) 'Promoting participation through community work', in L. Smith and D. Jones (eds) *Deprivation, participation and community action*, London: Routledge and Kegan Paul.

Tajfel, H. (1981) *Human groups and social categories: Studies in social psychology*, Cambridge: Cambridge University Press.

Taket, A. and White, L. (1997) 'Working with heterogeneity', *Systems Research and Behavioural Science*, vol 14, no 2, pp 101-11.

Tannen, D. (1992) *You just don't understand: Women and men in conversation*, London: Virago.

Tarrow, S. (1994) *Power in movement: Social movements, collective action and politics*, Cambridge: Cambridge University Press.

Tasker, L. (1975) 'Politics, theory and community work', in D. Jones and M. Mayo (eds) *Community work two*, London: Routledge and Kegan Paul.

Taylor, M. (1995a) 'Community work and the state: the changing context of UK practice', in G. Craig and M. Mayo (eds) *Community and empowerment: A reader in participation and development*, London: Zed Books.

Taylor, M. (1995b) *Unleashing the potential: Bringing residents to the centre of estate regeneration*, York: Joseph Rowntree Foundation.

Taylor, M. (1996) 'Between public and private: accountability in voluntary organisations', *Policy & Politics*, vol 24, no 1, pp 57-72.

Taylor, M. (1997) *The best of both worlds: The voluntary sector and local government*, York: Joseph Rowntree Foundation.

Taylor, M. (1998) 'Achieving community participation: the experience of resident involvement in urban regeneration in the UK', in D. Warburton (ed) *Community and sustainable development: Participation in the future*, London: Earthscan.

Taylor, M. (2000a) *Top down meets bottom up: Neighbourhood management*, York: Joseph Rowntree Foundation.

Taylor, M. (2000b) 'Communities in the lead: power, organisational capacity and social capital', *Urban Studies*, vol 37, pp 1019-35.

Taylor, M. (2003) *Public policy in the community*, Basingstoke: Palgrave Macmillan.

Taylor, M. and Hoggett, P. (1994) 'Trusting in networks? The third sector and welfare change', in P. Vidal and I. Vidal (eds) *Delivering welfare: Repositioning non-profit and co-operative action in western European welfare states*, Barcelona: CIES.

Taylor, M., Barr, A. and West, A. (2000) *Signposts to community development* (2nd edn), London: CDF.

Taylor, M., Langan, J. and Hoggett, P. (1995) *Encouraging diversity: Voluntary and private organisations in community care*, Aldershot: Arena.

Tebbutt, M. (1995) *Women's talk? Social history of gossip in working-class neighbourhoods*, Aldershot: Scholar Press.

Temple, J. (1998) *Social capability and economic growth*, Cambridge, MA: Harvard University Press.

Thomas, D. (1976) *Organising for social change: A study in the theory and practice of community work*, London: Allen and Unwin.

Thomas, D. (1983) *The making of community work*, London: Allen and Unwin.

Thomas, D. (1995) *Community development at work*, London: CDF.

Thompson, G., Frances, J., Levacic, R. and Mitchell, J. (eds) (1991) *Markets, hierarchies and networks: The co-ordination of social life*, London: Sage Publications.

Thompson, J.D. (1967) *Organisations in action*, New York, NY: McGraw-Hill.

Thompson, M. and Peebles-Wilkins, W. (1992) 'The impact of formal, informal and societal support networks on the psychological well-being of Black adolescent mothers', *Social Work*, vol 37, no 4, pp 322-8.

Thompson, N. (1998) *Promoting equality*, Basingstoke: Macmillan.

Tolsdorf, C. (1976) 'Social networks, support and coping; an exploratory study', *Family Relations*, vol 5, no 4, pp 407-18.

Tonkiss, F. and Passey, A. (1999) 'Trust, confidence and voluntary organisations: between values and institutions', *Sociology*, vol 33, no 2, pp 257-74, May.

Tönnies, F. (1887) *Community and association*, London: Routledge and Kegan Paul.

Too, L. (1997) *Feng shui fundamentals: Networking*, Shaftesbury: Element Books.

Trevillion, S. (1992) *Caring in the community: A networking approach to community partnership*, Harlow: Longmans.

Trist, E.L. (1983) 'Referent organisations and the development of inter-organisational domains', *Human Relations*, vol 36, pp 269-84.

Tudge, C. (1991) *Global ecology*, London: Natural History Museum.

Twelvetrees, A. (1976) *Community associations and centres: A comparative study*, Oxford: Pergamon Press.

Twelvetrees, A. (1982) *Community work* (1st edn), Basingstoke: Macmillan.

Twine, F. (1994) *Citizenship and social rights: The interdependence of self and society*, London: Sage Publications.

United Nations (1955) *Colonial handbook on community development*, London: HMSO.

Veale, A.M. (2000) 'Dilemmas of "community" in post-emergency Rwanda', *Community, Work and Family*, vol 3, no 3, pp 233-9.

Waddington, D., Wykes, K. and Critcher, C. (1991) *Split at the seams: Community, continuity and change after the 1984-5 coal strike*, Milton Keynes: Open University Press.

Waldrop, M.M. (1992) *Complexity: The emerging science at the edge of order and chaos*, New York, NY: Simon and Schuster.

Walker, P., Lewis, J., Lingayah, S. and Sommer, F. (2000) *Prove it! Measuring the effects of neighbourhood renewal on local people*, London: New Economics Foundation.

Wall, K. (1998) *Friendship skills and opportunities among people with learning disabilities*, Norwich: School of Social Work, University of East Anglia.

Wallman, S. (1986) 'Ethnicity and boundary process in context', in J. Rex and D. Mason (eds) *Theories of race and ethnic relations*, Cambridge: Cambridge University Press.

Warburton, D. (1998) 'A passionate dialogue: community and sustainable development', in D. Warburton (ed) *Community and sustainable development: Participation in the future*, London: Earthscan.

Ward, C. (1973) *Anarchy in action*, London: Allen and Unwin.

Warner, W.L. and Lunt, P.G. (1942) *The status system of a modern community*, New Haven, CT: Yale University Press.

Wasserman, S. and Faust, K. (1994) *Social network analysis*, Cambridge: Cambridge University Press.

Watt, S., Lea, M. and Spears, M. (2002) 'How social is internet communication? A reappraisal of bandwidth and anonymity effects', in S. Woolgar (ed) *Virtual society? Technology, cyberbole and reality*, Oxford: Oxford University Press.

WCAN (Warwickshire Community Action Network) (2002) *Networking or not working: A training resource pack*, Leamington Spa: Community Action Forum (Warwick District).

Webber, M.M. (1963) 'Order in diversity: community without propinquity', in W.J. Lowdon (ed) *Cities and space: The future use of urban land*, Baltimore, MD: Johns Hopkins Press.

Weber, M. (1930) *The protestant work ethic and the spirit of capitalism*, New York, NY: Scribner.

Weber, M. (1947) *The theory of social and economic organisation*, New York, NY: Free Press.

Weeks, J. (1990) 'The value of difference', in J. Rutherford (ed) *Identity: Community, culture, difference*, London: Lawrence and Wishart.

Wellman, B. (1979) 'The community question: the intimate networks of East Yorkers', *American Journal of Sociology*, vol 84, pp 1201-31.

Wellman, B. (1985) 'Domestic work, paid work and net work', in S. Duck and D. Perlman (eds) *Understanding personal relationships*, London: Sage Publications.

Wellman, B. (1999) 'The network community', in B. Wellman (ed) *Networks in the global village*, Boulder, CO: Westview Press.

Wellman, B. (2000) 'Network capital in a multi-level world: getting support from personal communities', in L. Nan, K. Cook and R. Burt (eds) *Social capital: Theory and Research*, Chicago, IL: Aldyne de Gruyter.

Wellman, B. and Gulia, M. (1999) 'Net-surfers don't ride alone: virtual communities as communities', in B. Wellman (ed) *Networks in the global village*, Boulder, CO: Westview Press.

Wellman, B. and Haythornthwaite, C. (eds) (2002) *The Internet in everyday life*, Oxford: Blackwell.

Werbner, P. (1988) 'Taking and giving: working women and female bonds in a Pakistani immigrant neighbourhood', in S. Westwood and P. Bhachu (eds) *Enterprising women: Ethnicity, economy and gender relations*, London: Routledge.

Werbner, P. (1990) *The migration process: Capital, gifts and offerings among British Pakistanis*, Oxford: Berg.

Wheatley, M.J. (1992) *Leadership in the new science: Learning about organisation from an orderly universe*, San Francisco, CA: Berrett-Koehler Publishers.

Wheeler, W. (1999) *A new modernity: Change in science, literature and politics*, London: Lawrence and Wishart.

White, H.C. (1963) *An anatomy of kinship*, Englewood Cliffs, NJ: Prentice-Hall.

White, L. (2001) 'Effective governance: complexity thinking and management science', *Systems Research and Behavioural Science*, vol 18, no 3, pp 241-57.

White, L.E. (1950) *Community or chaos*, London: National Council for Social Service.

Wilensky, H. (1967) *Organisational intelligence*, New York, NY: Basic Books.

Williams, C. and Windebank, J. (1995) 'Social polarisation of households in contemporary Britain: a whole economy perspective', *Regional Studies*, vol 29, no 8, pp 727-32.

Williams, C. and Windebank, J. (2000) 'Helping each other out?: community exchange in deprived neighbourhoods', *Community Development Journal*, vol 35, no 2, pp 146-56.

Williams, C., Lee, R., Leyshon, A. and Thrift, N. (2001) *Bridges into work: An evaluation of Local Exchange Trading Schemes (LETS)*, Bristol: The Policy Press.

Williams, G. (1973) 'Ways in for a community worker', *Talking Point* No 10, Newcastle-upon-Tyne: ACW.

Williams, P. (2002) 'The competent boundary spanner', *Public Administration*, vol 80, pp 103-24.

Williams, R. (1976) *Keywords: A vocabulary of culture and society*, Glasgow: Collins.

Williamson, O.E. (1973) 'Markets and hierarchies: some elementary considerations', *American Economic Review*, vol 63, pp 316-25.

Williamson, O.E. (1975) *Markets and hierarchies: Analysis and anti-trust implications*, New York, NY: Free Press.

Willmott, P. (1986) *Social networks, informal care and public policy*, London: Policy Studies Institute.

Wilson, E.O. (1992) *The diversity of life*, Cambridge, MA: Harvard University Press.

Wilson, E.O. (1998) *Consilience: The unity of knowledge*, London: Little, Brown and Company.

Wilson, M. and Wilde, P. (2001) *Building practitioner strengths*, London: CDF.

Wittenbaum, G.M. and Stasser, G. (1996) 'Management of information in small groups', in J.L. Nye and A.M. Brower (eds) *What's social about social cognition?*, Thousand Oaks, CA: Sage Publications.

Womankind Worldwide (2000) 'Exchanging skills and experiences', Newsletter, Winter.

Woolcock, M. (1998) 'Social capital and economic development: towards a theoretical synthesis and policy framework', *Theory and Society*, vol 27, pp 151-208.

Woolcock, M. (2001) 'The place of social capital in understanding social and economic outcomes', *ISUMA Canadian Journal of Policy Research*, vol 2, no 1, pp 11-17.

Yen, I. and Syme, S. (1999) 'The social environment and health: a discussion of the epidemiological literature', *Annual Review of Public Health*, vol 20, pp 287-308.

Yerkovich, S. (1977) 'Gossip as a way of speaking', *Journal of Communication*, vol 27, no 1, pp 192-6.

Young, M. and Willmott, P. (1957) *Family and kinship in East London*, London: Routledge and Kegan Paul.

Younghusband, E. (1968) *Community work and social change: A report on training*, London: Longman.

Zabrowitz, L.A. (1990) *Social perception*, Buckingham: Open University Press.

Zeldin, T. (1994) *An intimate history of humanity*, London: Sinclair-Stevenson.

Suggested further reading

Boissevain, J. (1974) *Friends of friends: Networks, manipulators and coalitions*, Oxford: Blackwell.

Castells, M. (2000) *The rise of the network society*, Oxford: Blackwell.

Cilliers, P. (1998) *Complexity and post-modernism*, London: Routledge.

Colebatch, H. and Lamour, P. (1993) *Market, bureaucracy and community*, London: Pluto Press.

Craig, G. and Mayo, M. (eds) (1995) *Community and empowerment*, London: Zed Books.

Crow, G. and Allan, G. (1994) *Community life*, Hemel Hempstead: Harvester Wheatsheaf.

Ebers, M. (2001) *The formation of inter-organisational networks*, Oxford: Oxford University Press.

Field, J. (2003) *Social capital*, London: Routledge.

Fischer, C. (1982) *To dwell amongst friends: Personal networks in town and city*, Chicago, IL: University of Chicago Press.

Gilchrist, A. (2001) *Community development and networking* (2nd edn), London: CDF.

Henderson, P. and Thomas, D. (2002) *Skills in neighbourhood work* (3rd edn), London: Allen and Unwin.

Hoggett, P. (ed) (1997) *Contested communities: Experiences, struggles, policies*, Bristol: The Policy Press.

Knoke, D. (1990) *Organising for collective action: The political economies of association*, New York, NY: Aldine de Gruyter.

Ledwith, M. (1997) *Participating in transformation: Towards a working model of community empowerment*, Birmingham: Venture Press.

Nash, V. (ed) (2002) *Reclaiming community*, London: IPPR.

Nohria, N. and Eccles, R.G. (eds) (1992) *Networks and organisations: Structure, form and action*, Boston, MA: Harvard Business School Press.

Taylor, M. (2003) *Public policy in the community*, Basingstoke: Palgrave Macmillan.

Index

Page numbers in *italics* refer to tables/figures